0069832

NEW DIRECTIONS FOR COMMUNITY COLLEGES

Arthur M. Cohen
EDITOR-IN-CHIEF

Florence B. Brawer
ASSOCIATE EDITOR

# Academic Advising: Organizing and Delivering Services for Student Success

Margaret C. King
*Schenectady County Commu*

*EDITOR*

Number 82, Summer 1993

JOSSEY-BASS PUBLISHERS
San Francisco

ACADEMIC ADVISING: ORGANIZING AND DELIVERING SERVICES FOR
STUDENT SUCCESS
*Margaret C. King* (ed.)
New Directions for Community Colleges, no. 82
Volume XXI, number 2
*Arthur M. Cohen,* Editor-in-Chief
*Florence B. Brawer,* Associate Editor

Microfilm copies of issues and articles are available in 16mm and 35mm,
as well as microfiche in 105mm, through University Microfilms Inc., 300
North Zeeb Road, Ann Arbor, Michigan 48106.

LC 85-644753          ISSN 0194-3081          ISBN 1-55542-687-5

NEW DIRECTIONS FOR COMMUNITY COLLEGES is part of The Jossey-Bass
Higher and Adult Education Series and is published quarterly by Jossey-
Bass Inc., Publishers, 350 Sansome Street, San Francisco, California
94104-1310 (publication number USPS 121-710) in association with the
ERIC Clearinghouse for Junior Colleges. Second-class postage paid at
San Francisco, California, and at additional mailing offices. POSTMASTER:
Send address changes to New Directions for Community Colleges,
Jossey-Bass Inc., Publishers, 350 Sansome Street, San Francisco, California
94104-1310.

SUBSCRIPTIONS for 1993 cost $48.00 for individuals and $70.00 for institutions, agencies, and libraries.

THE MATERIAL in this publication is based on work sponsored wholly or in
part by the Office of Educational Research and Improvement, U.S. Department of Education, under contract number RI-88-062002. Its contents do
not necessarily reflect the views of the Department, or any other agency of
the U.S. Government.

EDITORIAL CORRESPONDENCE should be sent to the Editor-in-Chief,
Arthur M. Cohen, at the ERIC Clearinghouse for Junior Colleges, University of California, Los Angeles, California 90024.

Cover photograph © Rene Sheret, After Image, Los Angeles, California,
1990.

# CONTENTS

# EDITOR'S NOTES

In recent years, academic advising has become recognized as a critical component of the educational services provided to students, and for good reason. Academic advising is the only structured service on college campuses that guarantees students interaction with concerned representatives of the institutions. Consequently, it can be viewed as the hub of the wheel, with connections to all of the other support services on campus. Effective advising can be a key factor in helping students make the necessary adjustments to college life and become integrated into the academic and social systems of our institutions. Such integration is directly linked to student success, satisfaction, and persistence.

To be effective, academic advising must be viewed as a developmental process, one that considers a student's life, career, and educational plans and goals prior to course selection and class scheduling. Wesley R. Habley and others have used the following definition of academic advising in presentations and workshops, and it is offered as a foundation for the chapters that follow: "Academic advising is a developmental process which assists students in the clarification of their life/career goals and in the development of educational plans for the realization of these goals. It is a decision-making process by which students realize their maximum educational potential through communication and information exchanges with an advisor; it is ongoing, multifaceted, and the responsibility of both student and advisor. The advisor serves as a facilitator of communication, a coordinator of learning experiences through course and career planning and academic progress review, and an agent of referral to other campus agencies as necessary" (Crockett, 1984, p. i).

This volume, *Academic Advising: Organizing and Delivering Services for Student Success*, begins with an in-depth discussion of developmental academic advising. Noting, in Chapter One, that "theory and practice are inseparable; practice is rooted in theory and theory informs practice" (p. 9), Thaddeus M. Raushi defines developmental advising and goes on to review the key developmental theories and to discuss their implications for advisers.

In Chapter Two, I discuss the critical role that academic advising can play in student retention and transfer. A summary of Tinto's (1987) model of student departure is followed by a review of some of the research that operationalized that model. Themes of attrition and the role that advisers play in each are also noted. The chapter concludes with a discussion of the importance of the transfer function and the role of advisers in enhancing transfer.

Wesley R. Habley describes the state of advising in community colleges in Chapter Three. Using data from the American College Testing Program's fourth national survey on academic advising (Habley, 1993), Habley describes organizational models that exist in two-year colleges as well as coordination and reporting lines, institutional policy statements, adviser training, adviser evaluation, recognition and reward, program goals, and program effectiveness.

A more detailed discussion of advising models and delivery systems is provided in Chapter Four. I describe the factors that influence the ways in which advising services can be organized and the seven different organizational models that exist, and I discuss the strengths and weaknesses of various advising delivery systems.

The next two chapters focus on key components of effective advising programs. In Chapter Five, Portia K. Weston discusses the importance of adviser training, noting that it both enables faculty and staff to develop as advisers and enhances communication within the institution. A model training program is presented. In Chapter Six, Buddy Ramos reviews important factors in designing and implementing an evaluation program, describes a specific model, and offers suggestions for implementation of a recognition and reward program.

In Chapter Seven, Judith L. Sanford-Harris offers general considerations and strategies for advising the two-year college student. Thomas Brown and Mario Rivas follow in Chapter Eight with a discussion on advising multicultural students. Growing out of a presentation to the Maricopa Community College District in Tempe, Arizona, their chapter describes the challenges faced by effective multicultural and pluralistic advisers and offers a specific intervention strategy.

A summary of critical advising times and suggested intervention strategies is provided by Martha T. Garing in Chapter Nine. In Chapter Ten, Karin Petersen Hsiao concludes this volume with an annotated bibliography of selected sources of information related to academic advising in the community college setting.

Special thanks are extended to two Schenectady County Community College colleagues for their assistance in the preparation of this volume: Thaddeus M. Raushi, who served as editor for the editor, and Jan Orlowski, without whom this volume would never have been completed.

Margaret C. King
Editor

## References

Crockett, D. S. *Advising Skills, Techniques, and Resources.* Iowa City, Iowa: American College Testing, 1984.

Habley, W. R. *Fulfilling the Promise?* Iowa City, Iowa: American College Testing, 1993.

Tinto, V. *Leaving College: Rethinking the Causes and Cures of Student Attrition.* Chicago: University of Chicago Press, 1987. 246 pp. (ED 283 416)

MARGARET C. KING *is assistant dean for student development at Schenectady County Community College, Schenectady, New York. She was a founding member of the National Academic Advising Association and serves as its president (1991 to 1993). She has been a faculty member at the American College Testing/NACADA Summer Institute on Academic Advising and serves as a consultant on academic advising in two-year colleges.*

*Developmental advising is a process shaped, nurtured, and defined by both traditional and newly emerging theory, reflecting psychosocial, cognitive, ecological, and student-specific orientations.*

# Developmental Academic Advising

*Thaddeus M. Raushi*

The notion of developmental academic advising embraces myriad concepts and theories, drawing on disciplines of human development and education. Although relatively short in history, its roots are deeply planted in educational objectives that focus on wholeness as well as student diversity. And this diversity is no more keenly experienced in higher education than in the two-year college sector. There, society's multiethnic and multicultural heritages, age and gender differences, and socioeconomic and class variations are engaged together in the process of higher learning. It is within this complexity of human society and student differences that developmental academic advising serves a critical role in helping two-year colleges meet the challenges of and demands for quality education in the 1990s.

Quality advising impacts both on the student and the college community in general. Habley and Crockett (1988, p. 11) have written that "students who formulate a sound educational/career plan based on their values, interests, and abilities will have an increased chance for academic success, satisfaction, and persistence." Greenwood (1984, p. 64) has suggested that quality advisement "promotes the creation of a caring environment, builds a positive public image, enhances students' development, fosters a better understanding of academic and administrative processes, rewards advisors for their work and produces primary and secondary benefits to society." Quality advising fosters student development and at the same time enriches the academic community, the adviser, and the society at large. Greenwood goes on to note that "academic advising is probably the single most educational activity that all students experience as they move through college" (pp. 64–65). Within most colleges, there already exists some form of advising structure that can provide a means for reaching out to all students. The relevant question thus concerns the nature of the advisement process and the vision and commitment of the institution to a comprehensive quality model.

Developmental advising is an approach that results in quality advisement. But what is the nature and character of developmental academic advising? What generates and nurtures this form of advising? In addressing these questions, this chapter provides a framework within which to explore implications of developmental advising for student retention, for advisement delivery systems, for strategies in working with the two-year college student, and for an intrusive approach to the advising process.

## Developmental Advising Defined

Developmental advising is rooted in beliefs about human development and the systems within which humans interact. The definition of developmental advising emerges from an understanding of advising as a process and as an orientation, experienced within the context of multiple life and college systems.

**Process and Orientation.** Developmental advising is, first, a *process*, that is, to use a dictionary definition, "something going on or proceeding." As such, this form of advising reflects the idea of movement, of progression. It goes beyond signing a form or providing information to enhancing the process of student growth. In his "scheme of development" on patterns of thought and meaning making in lives of college students, Perry (1981, p. 78) has noted that it is the actual movement or "transition" between stages that is developmental, not simply the stage itself. This movement is student development.

Perry (1981, p. 97) has also suggested that growth and development within this process can be recursive, although "the 'same' issues, faced over and over again, may not really be the same." Recognition of this dimension in the growth process may be especially meaningful in the advising of older college students. Older students often explore issues that were faced earlier in their lives but are later addressed within the context of a broader life experience and, therefore, are not really the same issues.

Further, developmental advising is more accurately understood as an *orientation* rather than a method or system. It is essentially the viewing of advisement within a theoretical frame of reference that is developmental in nature. Human beings act from some set of meanings about what goes on around them; advisers advise from whatever sets of meanings they have adopted regarding students, students' needs, and the two-year college. Developmental advising proceeds from a set of meanings that reflects a developmental understanding of people and systems.

**Context.** To advise from a developmental perspective is to view students at work on life tasks in the context of their whole life settings, including their college experience. It is an ecological perspective that recognizes the importance of interactions between the student and the campus environment, a type of "campus ecology" (Banning, 1989). Egan and Cowan (1979, p. 6) used the Lewinian concept that "behavior is a function of interaction between person and environment" to develop a human service/education model for working with people. They proposed that "human development is a function of the interaction between people (P) and the human systems (S) in which they are involved, and of the interaction of these systems with one another" (p. 6). They went on to suggest that "any approach to meeting the developmental needs of people must keep individuals and the systems in which they live in focus simultaneously" (p. 13).

Within the two-year college, there are many internal systems (for example, the faculty, student government, the advising system, student development, administration, and departments). There are also external systems that interact with the college systems (for example, the business community, four-year colleges, accreditation bodies, welfare agencies, student's peer group, employment setting, and family). How these various systems support, conflict, network, compete, and generally interact with the two-year college, with one another, and with the student affects how the student develops. Adapting Egan and Cowan's (1979) terminology to the field of academic advising, we might call this ecological perspective a "student-in-systems" view. Within this view, the adviser may also be part of several systems while at the same time experiencing her or his own developmental life tasks and issues. And it is from this student-in-systems perspective that the interaction between advisee, adviser, and various systems emerges as the context in which developmental advising is both formed and conducted.

**Definition.** The nature of developmental advising reflects the characteristics and nature of human development in general. Miller and McCaffrey (1982, p. 21) identified four basic principles common to human development: Human development is continuous in nature, human development is cumulative in nature, human development follows a simple-to-complex continuum, human development tends to be orderly and stage-related.

These principles inform the advising process with respect to the progressive nature of the student's development as a total person and the potential impact and value of life experiences on this process. Developmental advising focuses on the whole person and works with the student at that person's own life stage of development. Ender, Winston, and Miller (1982, pp. 7–8) identified characteristics of developmental advising that embrace these principles and define the developmental orientation of this process:

"Developmental advising is a process. . . . [It is] continuous and established on the basis of the advisor-advisee relationship."

"Developmental advising is concerned with human growth. . . . [The growth is] cognitive, affective, career, physical, and moral."

"Developmental advising is goal related and its goals are central to its purpose . . . collaboratively established they are owned by the advisee."

"Developmental advising requires establishment of a caring human relationship."

"Advisors serve as adult role models and mentors. . . . The advisor reflects for the student both the image of a faculty/staff member and the philosophy of the institution."

"Developmental advising is the cornerstone of collaboration between academic and student affairs."

"Developmental advising utilizes all campus and community resources. . . . Advisors serve as the hub of students' learning experiences."

Developmental advising is both goal-centered and student-ownership-based. Goal-centered advising engages the student in the tasks of identifying and setting goals as well as in taking action toward those goals. This goal-centered dimension encompasses the three tasks of (1) exploring, (2) deciding, and (3) step taking. Through the process of accomplishing these tasks, students are empowered to take rightful ownership of both the process and the outcome. In researching what students want from advising, Winston and Sandor (1984, p. 12) found that "woven throughout is the underlying theme that students wish to be considered partners in the advising process, not the recipients of advice."

Developmental advising is also a collaborative endeavor of academic and student affairs. Though these divisions often function independently, a developmental advising process draws jointly on these education areas and professionals in addressing student development needs. Ender, Winston, and Miller (1982, p. 4) "take strong exception to the dualistic approach to educating the whole person and believe that the integration of personality and intellectual development is an essential and viable goal of higher education," and they call for the integration of academic and student affairs in the process.

Ender, Winston, and Miller's use of the term *adult* in relation to role model and mentor might better be understood in the two-year college context in terms of "professional educator." Within a student population where the advisee is often older than the adviser, the maturity suggested by the term *adult* concerns the judgment and support that most students seek from a professional educator. Winston and Sandor (1984, p. 12) have noted that "advisors are seen primarily as persons who teach and support students, but allow them maximum freedom of behavior and decision-making." This is the role of a mature educator, no matter his or her age status.

Among the many definitions of developmental advising, Crockett and

Habley (1987, p. 9) have provided a comprehensive, working characterization of the process, adaptable to various settings of higher education: "Academic advising is a developmental process which assists students in the clarification of their life/career goals and in the development of educational plans for the realization of these goals. It is a decision-making process by which students realize their maximum educational potential through communication and information exchanges with an advisor; it is ongoing, multifaceted, and the responsibility of both student and advisor. The advisor serves as a facilitator of communication, a coordinator of learning experiences through course and career planning and academic progress review, and an agent of referral to other campus agencies as necessary." This definition incorporates the various elements of human development, systems, and the interaction of people-in-systems. It serves to define the developmental orientation of advising, as discussed in this chapter as well as in the other chapters of this book.

## Developmental Theories and Their Implications

Theory and practice are inseparable; practice is rooted in theory and theory informs practice. Although some take the value of theory lightly, everyone uses theory. Anyone who gives an opinion or makes a decision theorizes about the information at hand. Reid and Smith (1989 p. 46) have observed that "theory is a system of concepts and hypotheses that attempt to define, explain, and predict phenomena." The very nature of this definition suggests, for the academic adviser, that theory can provide an understanding of the student and of systems and offer direction in making decisions about the nature of service. For example, knowledge about developmental needs of a forty-year-old displaced homemaker may suggest approaches to course decision making or career planning that differ from those most effective with a recent high school graduate living at home with full parental support. Theory can "enable the practitioner to comprehend and describe aspects of reality that otherwise might be difficult to order or that might escape attention altogether" as well as "provide the 'whys' of problems and behavior and the rationale for intervention" (Reid and Smith, 1989, pp. 46). Developmental advising has found its basis and nurturance in a multitude of theories of human and student development (Ender, Winston, and Miller, 1982; Miller and McCaffrey, 1982; Thomas and Chickering, 1984). Stage (1991, pp. 57–58) has proposed that from this broad array of theories there emerge three elements of commonality useful to the educator in applying theory to practice: (1) Focus on the individual: "The major student development theories are psychologically based. As such, the focus is on individual change during the college years." (2) Dependence-independence-autonomy continuum: "Many student development theories focus on students' attempts to achieve a balance between dependence and autonomy." (3) <u>Challenge and support</u>: "Many student development theorists and researchers agree on the importance of challenge to the student accompanied by support within the environment." These common themes, prevalent throughout most of the theories and typologies, shape the adviser's developmental understanding of students and student growth.

Theories related to the development of students have been organized and clustered in various ways. One approach is presented by Upcraft (1989) in relation to first-year college students. Upcraft's framework of theories commonly applied to student development is organized in terms of traditional students, nontraditional students, and college students in general. Reframing and expanding on his work, I suggest that college academic advisers might best view development theories in terms of two categories: basic versus focused. Basic theories address psychosocial, cognitive-behavioral, and ecological (person-environment interaction) factors. Focused theories, of more recent emergence, address specific populations, such as adult students and women. This brief synopsis of select theories provides only a cursory exposure to the broad theory base of developmental advising; the chapter's source citations constitute a point of departure for more intensive investigation of individual theories.

**Basic Theories.** The classification of basic theories includes those theories that foster an understanding of college students from a broad human development perspective.

*Psychosocial.* The psychoanalytic theory of Freud has a developmental emphasis that focuses attention on internal human processes as the key influences in personality and behavior. Erikson (1963) expanded this developmental thinking by recognizing the importance of the person's conscious self in relation to behavior and sense of personal identity. His eight ages, or psychosocial stages, introduced the concept of continuous development over the life span. While Stage 5 (identity versus role confusion) is most often associated with college students, Stages 6–8 (intimacy versus isolation, generativity versus stagnation, and ego integrity versus despair) merit attention, especially as the number of older students increases in the college population.

Sanford (1967) envisioned the psychosocial development of students as an ongoing process of both integration and differentiation. Student growth is realized as this process unfolds through the student's interaction with the college environment. Sanford suggested that "a person develops through being challenged: for change to occur, there must be internal or external stimuli which upset his existing equilibrium, which cause instability that existing modes of adaptation do not suffice to correct, and which thus require the person to make new responses and so to expand his personality" (1967, p. 51). As an integral part of the student's college environment, the adviser can play a significant role by encouraging those experiences and interactions that stimulate the student "to make new responses" (p. 51) and thereby grow.

A widely recognized framework for understanding student change from a psychosocial development perspective has been formulated by Chickering (1969), who conceived of seven distinct areas, or vectors, of development. These vectors describe various dimensions of student growth: (1) achieving competence: development of intellectual, physical, manual, social, and interpersonal skills; (2) managing emotions: awareness of emotions and appropriate and effective means of expression; (3) becoming autonomous: recognition and acceptance of interdependence as an aspect of becoming emotionally and instrumentally independent; (4) establishing identity: development of a sense of self, sense of physical being, and sexual identity; (5) freeing interpersonal relationships: development of a responsive tolerance of others, quality in intimate relationships, and capacity for increased trust, independence, and individuality; (6) clarifying purposes: development of life purposes inclusive of avocational and vocational dreams and plans as well as a general life-style; (7) developing integrity: clarification of a set of beliefs that are consistent with the inner person and that serve to guide the individual's behavior (1969, pp. 8–19).

Each vector can be translated into concrete areas of student growth, including specifically defined behaviors. Approaches, programs, or activities may be designed to foster development of these behaviors. Measurable student outcomes can then be formulated, an issue of increasing importance within higher education. The adviser may use the seven-vectors theory in conjunction with focused theories, which address specific student populations, as a viable tool for helping define and nurture developmental advising tasks.

*Cognitive-Developmental.* Ego, moral, and cognitive-ethical development are human dimensions that have direct relevance to the advising process. Loevinger (1976) identified a set of self-defining sequential stages through which the individual moves in the development of ego: presocial, symbiotic, impulsive, self-protective, conformist, conscientious-conformist (a stage of transition), conscientious, individualistic, autonomous, and integrated. The stages are not rigid and reflect characteristics true of everyone to varying degrees: "What changes during the course of ego development is a complex interwoven fabric of impulse control, character, interpersonal relations, conscious preoccupations, and cognitive complexity, among other things" (Loevinger, 1976, p. 26).

Kohlberg's (1984) cognitive-developmental theory of moralization identifies six distinct stages, within three developmental levels, through which moral judgment progresses. Kohlberg suggested that from a "social perspective" these stages entail a move from an egocentric view of self and others to "the perspective of an individual who has made the moral commitments or holds the standards on which a good or just society must be based" (1984, p. 178).

Both Loevinger and Kohlberg presented theories that are rich in value in terms of an understanding of a person's ego and moral judgment development during his or her college experience. Readiness to explore, understand, and draw from academic and social learning may depend on where the student is at in ego and moral judgment development. The adviser can play a significant role in enhancing the student's development by encouraging new experiences, working with career planning and other areas of decision making, and actively supporting a college environment that is conducive to student growth.

The scheme of cognitive and ethical development presented by Perry (1981) has been widely adapted as a model of student development. The theory incorporates positions of cognitive development and transitional phases across the positions. In mapping this detailed scheme, Perry suggested four broad categories for making meaning of the positions: (1) dualism: "division of meaning into two realms—Good versus Bad, Right versus Wrong, We versus They, All that is not Success is Failure, and the like"; (2) multiplicity: "diversity of opinion and values is recognized as legitimate in areas where right answers are not yet known"; (3) relativism: "diversity of opinion, values, and judgment derived from coherent sources, evidence, logic, systems, and patterns allowing for analysis and comparison"; (4) commitment: "an affirmation, choice or decision . . . made in the awareness of Relativism" (1981, pp. 79–80). Perry also identified three ways of understanding how some students may redirect their movement through the positions: (1) temporizing: "postponement of movement for a year or more"; (2) escape: "alienation, abandonment of responsibility, Exploitation of Multiplicity and Relativism for avoidance of Commitment"; (3) retreat: "avoidance of complexity and ambivalence by regression to Dualism colored by hatred of otherness" (p. 80).

For the academic adviser, awareness of a student's location in this cognitive and ethical development scheme can aid in understanding the student's reactions and responses to college and other experiences. The scheme may further suggest steps to be taken in various facets of the student's educational planning. A student in the simplistic dualism phase, for example, will be much more resistant to understanding cultural pluralism and the value of intercultural programs than will the student who is in the relativism phase of development. One's approach to encouraging students' exposure to such programs as part of their learning experience may, therefore, take on different forms for different students.

Drawing both on psychosocial and cognitive-developmental theories, Miller and McCaffrey (1982) introduced a framework around which an effective developmental academic advising program might be modeled. Called "Spice of Developmental Life," this "thematic framework of advising establishes that the self, the physical, the interpersonal, the career, and the educational are all essential aspects of human development and must therefore be considered as important to any developmental advising program" (1982, p. 25). Miller and McCaffrey have provided a prime example of how multiple theories can be integrated to create a comprehensive basis for establishing and conducting an advising program with a developmental orientation.

*Person-Environment Interaction.* As discussed earlier, the context in which developmental advising happens has impact on the content and quality of the advising. Egan and Cowan's (1979) formulation of human development as a function of the interaction between the individual and systems provides a theoretical base for understanding the important role of systems within the college environment in either empowering or retarding students' growth. Theories such as Moos's (1976) social-ecological approach to demonstrating the impact of milieus and Holland's (1985) typology of personalities as related to occupational environments underscore the importance of the relationship between the setting and student growth. Holland's work further aids advisers as they guide students in their career decision making. Using the six personality types (realistic, investigative, artistic, social, enterprising, and conventional), advisers can help students discover meaningful "fits" between themselves and career pathways.

Bronfenbrenner (1979, p. 27) has stated that "development never takes place in a vacuum; it is always embedded and expressed through behavior in a particular environmental context." This "ecological environment is conceived as a set of nested structures, each inside the next" (p. 3), structures called the micro-, meso-, exo-, and macrosystems. Envisioned as a set of concentric circles, within the college context, the innermost core is the individual student; the outer circles might progressively include the activities and interpersonal relations within the setting of the specific college (for example, learner, adviser-student relationship, club member) as the microsystem; the interrelationships of the settings of which the student is a part (for example, college, family, work, community and social life) as the mesosystem; external systems in which the student is not an active participant but that affect the student's setting and experience (for example, the college's funding source, parent's workplace, spouse's job, child's school) as the exosystem; and the beliefs, cultures, and ideologies that affect the nature and content of the settings or inner circles (for example, society's value of a college education, belief in equal rights) as the macrosystem.

The student's development as a whole person is a function of the interaction of this complex set of systems. As a student's role changes upon entering the college or while in the college or upon departing, the transition is a point of tension and stress (Banning, 1989). These transitions, though, hold the potential for student learning and growth. While no academic adviser can begin to unfold this complexity of interactions, an understanding of this framework can provide insight into the student, the student's life situation, and the implications for adviser or student actions in advancing student learning and development.

**Focused Theories.** In addition to basic theories, developmental advising also draws on theories focused on specific populations.

*Adult Learners.* One population common to the two-year college sector is composed of individuals older than traditional college-age students. While basic theories have application to adult students, special attention has been given to understanding the unique character of the adult learner in higher education (K. Cross, 1981; Knowles, 1984; Knox, 1977). Knowles (1984) has presented an androgynous orientation to understanding the adult learner and his or her process of learning. This orientation is a reflection of the following assumptions about adult learners, assumptions that can be useful to the developmental academic adviser in the two-year college setting: (1) Need to know: "Adults need to know why they need to learn something before undertaking to learn it." (2) Learners' self-concept: "Adults have a self-concept of being responsible for their own decisions, for their own lives." (3) Role of the learners' experience: "Adults come into an educational activity with both a greater volume and a different quality of experience from youths." (4) Readiness to learn: "Adults become ready to learn those things they need to know and be able to do in order to cope effectively with their real-life situations." (5) Orientation to learning: "In contrast to children's and youths' subject-centered orientation to learning (at least in school), adults are life-centered (or task-centered or problem-centered) in their orientation to learning." (6) Motivation: "While adults are responsive to some external motivators (better jobs, promotions, higher salaries, and the like), the most potent motivators are internal pressures (the desire for increased job satisfaction, self-esteem, quality of life, and the like)" (Knowles, 1984, pp. 55–61).

Three adult transitional periods are identified by Levinson (1978) in his study of adult men: early adult transition (seventeen to twenty-two years); midlife transition (forty to forty-five); and late adult transition (sixty to sixty-five). Although ages are specified, they may vary; most important is the recognition that these transitional periods exist between the more stable periods of adolescence and early adulthood, early and middle life, and middle and late life, respectively. This awareness may guide advisers in their understanding of the developmental tasks in which older students might be engaged while pursuing a college education.

*Women.* Earlier theories of development and identity formation have been commonly applied to all persons, though many theories were formulated from the study of males (for example, Perry studied a group of male Harvard students; Kohlberg, a group of boys; and Levinson, forty adult males). More recently, theories or models have been based on the study of women (Gilligan, 1982; Belenky, Clinchy, Goldberger, and Tarule, 1986) and have provided new insights into both women's development in particular and human development in general. The earlier, more traditional theories identified healthy development and identity with "autonomy and separation." The more recent models identify the value and role of connect-edness and relationships (Enns, 1991), two concepts that have been viewed as weaknesses in the more traditional theories. Gilligan (1982, p. 18) has observed that "the very traits that traditionally have defined the 'goodness' of women, their care for and sensitivity to the needs of others, are those that mark them as deficient in moral development." From Gilligan's perspective, connectedness and relationship are "themes" (as opposed to gender-specific traits) that one uses in defining the self, just as are autonomy and separation. These themes provide different routes in the process of development, but each contributes to the growth of the whole person; "these disparate visions in their tension reflect the paradoxical truths of human experience—that we know ourselves as separate only insofar as we live in connection with others, and that we experience relationship only insofar as we differentiate other from self" (1982, p. 63).

Through in-depth interviews with women, Belenky, Clinchy, Gold-berger, and Tarule (1986, p. 3) examined "women's ways of knowing and describe five different perspectives from which women view reality and draw conclusions about truth, knowledge, and authority": (1) silence: absence of an outer vantage point from which to see one's whole self and ab-sence of a belief in one's capability to learn; (2) received knowledge: taking in knowledge of others (equating the voice of authority to truth) with little belief in one's own ability to speak with a voice; (3) subjective knowledge: developing a private and subjective view of truth, coming from within the self, and a foundation of knowledge from which one can explore the surrounding world; (4) procedural knowledge: developing procedures and skills for communicating with a voice of reason from either a separate knowing perspective or a connected knowing perspective (separate or connected as defined in terms of the relationship between the knower and the object of knowing); and (5) constructed knowledge: integrating knowl-edge that is realized intuitively and that has been learned from others, subjective knowing, and objective knowing.

The concluding lessons learned by Belenky, Clinchy, Goldberger, and Tarule (1986, p. 229) from their extensive study of women have direct relevance to higher education: "Educators can help women develop their own authentic voices if they emphasize connection over separation, under-standing and acceptance over assessment, and collaboration over debate; if they accord respect to and allow time for the knowledge that emerges from firsthand experience; if instead of imposing their own expectation and arbitrary requirements, they encourage students to evolve their own pat-terns of work based on the problems they are pursuing." Developmental advisers can draw on this theoretical framework as they establish relation-ships with students, assist with career and education planning, provide encouragement and challenge, and work toward influencing change in the college systems.

*People of Color.* Student development in a predominantly white education institution is shaped essentially by Euro-American values (McEwen,
Roper, Bryant, and Langa, 1990). Two-year colleges basically share this
same value system with other sectors of higher education, though they are
often found on the forefront of addressing educational needs of people of
color. Wright (1987, p. 10) has contended that "little attention has been
given to 'culture-specific' aspects of development," a major weakness when
applying theory to nondominant student populations. "To understand
minority students' development thoroughly requires an examination of
social environmental factors, such as economics (especially poverty), ethnic
or cultural background, and racial and gender bias and their interactive
effects on American society and on minority college student's growth"
(p. 11). Advisers who serve people of color need to be sensitive to these
areas when addressing student needs and working with students in decision
making and other tasks. Advisers may also enhance their effectiveness
through continued growth in their own multicultural awareness.

In designing a developmental orientation sensitive to working with
people of color, McEwen, Roper, Bryant, and Langa (1990, p. 430) provided
one example of areas to be considered. They delineated nine factors related
to developmental tasks for African Americans, which call for understanding
from a culture-specific perspective: developing ethnic and racial identity,
interacting with the dominant culture, developing cultural aesthetics and
awareness, developing identity, developing interdependence, fulfilling af-
filiation needs, surviving intellectually, developing spiritually, and developing social responsibility. Although designed specifically for African American
students, these factors merit cross-cultural consideration. In addition, it is
important to note that, as with most groupings of people, there is heteroge-
neity among individuals; "because of the diversity in the Black community,
there is no such thing as a 'typical Black person' " (McEwen, Roper, Bryant,
and Langa, 1990, p. 434).

An understanding of the process of development of racial identity can
further add to an adviser's work with people of color. W. Cross (1978,
pp. 16–18) has delineated stages through which a person develops in the
process of acquiring a racial identity: (1) preencounter stage: holding on
to the old identity or frame of reference to be changed; (2) encounter stage:
separating from an old worldview and receptive to a new identity; (3)
immersion-emersion stage: excited about and struggling to clarify the new
identity, with some possible militantism; (4) internalization stage: moving
toward a pluralistic perspective; and (5) internalization-commitment stage:
internalized new identity and actively involved in working toward resolu-
tions to the "new group" problems. Advisers benefit both from multicultural
perspectives on developmental issues as well as from recognition of the
existence of stages in identity development related to race, culture, or both.

The application of a stage model can help advisers better understand behaviors as well as support and empower students in their identity development.

*Lesbians and Gay Men.* The development of an identity as a lesbian or as a gay man takes on dimensions not addressed adequately by traditional theories of development. Cass's (1979) model of homosexual identity formation draws on the individual's perception of her or his own behaviors and the consequences of these behaviors. The model suggests six stages through which a person moves in arriving at an integration of sexual orientation and self-concept: (1) identity confusion: recognizes that her or his behavior can be identified as homosexual; (2) identity comparison: aware of differences in perceptions between self and others and the resulting alienation; (3) identity tolerance: tolerates but does not accept homosexual identity, though seeks out other lesbians or gay men to deal with feelings of alienation; (4) identity acceptance: accepts homosexuality as a way of life, interacting both with lesbians and gay men and with the heterosexually oriented institutions; (5) identity pride: revalues homosexual others more positively, acquires a strong sense of pride, and may move to activism in the systems; and (6) identity synthesis: no longer a "we-they" relationship with heterosexuals; maximum congruence between the personal and public self (1979, pp. 219–235).

Troiden (1989, pp. 50–68) has drawn on sociological perspectives in presenting another theoretical framework for understanding the stages through which a person moves in developing an identity as a lesbian or gay man: (1) sensitization: homosexuality is not personally relevant; (2) identity confusion: inner turmoil regarding sexual identity; may deny, attempt to repair, or avoid dealing with his or her identity; (3) identity assumption: becomes a self-identity and an identity presented to other lesbians and gay men; and (4) commitment: adopts homosexuality as a way of life within own self and publicly. Incorporated with traditional theories of development, this model and Cass's (1979) model provide the adviser with insights into the process of developing a lesbian or gay identity while simultaneously experiencing other dimensions of human growth. This process may hold not only for the younger, traditional age student but also for the older student who, later in life, is welcoming the support for openly expressing her or his sexual preference and identity.

## Conclusion

Developmental advising is a comprehensive, collaborative, and empowering process toward maximization of the student's educational potential. It is developmental in that students are viewed from a set of meanings that entail a developmental understanding of people and systems. The theory that enlightens, shapes, and nurtures developmental advising reflects psycho-social, cognitive-behavioral, environmental, and population-specific orientations.

Implications of theory for developmental advising within two-year colleges are the central topic of this chapter. Applications and challenges for advancing and implementing this quality advising process are the topics of the remaining chapters in this volume.

## References

Banning, J. H. "Impact of College Environments on Freshman Students." In M. L. Upcraft, J. N. Gardner, and Associates, *The Freshman Year Experience: Helping Students Survive and Succeed in College.* San Francisco: Jossey-Bass, 1989.

Belenky, M. F., Clinchy, B. M., Goldberger, N. R., and Tarule, J. M. *Women's Ways of Knowing: The Development of Self, Voice, and Mind.* New York: Basic Books, 1986.

Bronfenbrenner, U. *The Ecology of Human Development: Experiments by Nature and Design.* Cambridge, Mass.: Harvard University Press, 1979.

Cass, V. C. "Homosexual Identity Formation: A Theoretical Model." *Journal of Homosexuality,* 1979, 4 (3), 219–235.

Chickering, A. W. *Education and Identity.* San Francisco: Jossey-Bass, 1969.

Crockett, D. S., and Habley, W. R. *Academic Advising Conference Outline and Notes.* Iowa City, Iowa: American College Testing, 1987.

Cross, K. P. *Adults as Learners: Increasing Participation and Facilitating Learning.* San Francisco: Jossey-Bass, 1981.

Cross, W. E., Jr. "The Thomas and Cross Models of Psychological Nigrescence: A Literature Review." *Journal of Black Psychology,* 1978, 5 (1), 13–31.

Egan, G., and Cowan, M. *People in Systems: A Model for Development in the Human Service Professions and Education.* Monterey, Calif.: Brooks/Cole, 1979.

Ender, S. C., Winston, R. B., Jr., and Miller, T. K. "Academic Advising as Student Development." In R. B. Winston, Jr., S. C. Ender, and T. K. Miller (eds.), *Developmental Approaches to Academic Advising.* New Directions for Student Services, no. 17. San Francisco: Jossey-Bass, 1982.

Enns, C. Z. "The 'New' Relationship Models of Women's Identity: A Review and Critique for Counselors." *Journal of Counseling and Development,* 1991, 69 (3), 209–217.

Erikson, E. H. *Childhood and Society.* (2nd ed.) New York: Norton, 1963.

Gilligan, C. *In a Different Voice: Psychological Theory and Women's Development.* Cambridge, Mass.: Harvard University Press, 1982.

Greenwood, J. D. "Academic Advising and Institutional Goals: A President's Perspective." In R. B. Winston, Jr., and others, *Developmental Academic Advising: Addressing Students' Educational, Career, and Personal Needs.* San Francisco: Jossey-Bass, 1984.

Habley, W. R., and Crockett, D. S. "The Third ACT National Survey of Academic Advising." In W. R. Habley (ed.), *The Status and Future of Academic Advising: Problems and Promise.* Iowa City, Iowa: American College Testing, 1988.

Holland, J. *Making Vocational Choices: A Theory of Vocational Personalities and Work Environments.* (2nd ed.) Englewood Cliffs, N.J.: Prentice Hall, 1985.

Knowles, M. S. *The Adult Learner: A Neglected Species.* (3rd ed.) Houston: Gulf, 1984.

Knox, A. B. *Adult Development and Learning: A Handbook on Individual Growth and Competence in the Adult Years.* San Francisco: Jossey-Bass, 1977.

Kohlberg, L. *The Psychology of Moral Development: The Nature and Validity of Moral Stages.* San Francisco: Harper & Row, 1984.

Levinson, D. J. *The Seasons of a Man's Life.* New York: Ballantine Books, 1978.

Loevinger, J. *Ego Development: Conceptions and Theories.* San Francisco: Jossey-Bass, 1976.

McEwen, M. K., Roper, L. D., Bryant, D. R., and Langa, M. J. "Incorporating the Development of African-American Students into Psychosocial Theories of Student Development." *Journal of College Student Development,* 1990, *31* (5), 429–436.

Miller, T. K., and McCaffrey, S. S. "Student Development Theory: Foundations for Academic Advising." In R. B. Winston, Jr., S. C. Ender, and T. K. Miller (eds.), *Developmental Approaches to Academic Advising.* New Directions for Student Services, no. 17. San Francisco: Jossey-Bass, 1982.

Moos, R. H. *The Human Context: Environmental Determinants of Behavior.* New York: Wiley, 1976.

Perry, W. G., Jr. "Cognitive and Ethical Growth: The Making of Meaning." In A. W. Chickering and Associates, *The Modern American College: Responding to the New Realities of Diverse Students and a Changing Society.* San Francisco: Jossey-Bass, 1981.

Reid, W. J., and Smith, A. D. *Research in Social Work.* (2nd ed.) New York: Columbia University Press, 1989.

Sanford, N. *Where Colleges Fail: A Study of the Student as a Person.* San Francisco: Jossey-Bass, 1967.

Stage, F. K. "Common Elements of Theory: A Framework for College Student Development." *Journal of College Student Development,* 1991, *32* (1), 56–61.

Thomas, R. E., and Chickering, A. W. "Foundations for Academic Advising." In R. B. Winston, Jr., and others, *Developmental Academic Advising: Addressing Students' Educational, Career, and Personal Needs.* San Francisco: Jossey-Bass, 1984.

Troiden, R. R. "The Formation of Homosexual Identities." *Journal of Homosexuality,* 1989, *17* (1–2), 43–73.

Upcraft, M. L. "Understanding Student Development: Insights from Theory." In M. L. Upcraft, J. N. Gardner, and Associates, *The Freshman Year Experience: Helping Students Survive and Succeed in College.* San Francisco: Jossey-Bass, 1989.

Winston, R. B., Jr., and Sandor, J. A. "Developmental Academic Advising: What Do Students Want?" *National Academic Advising Association Journal,* 1984, *4* (1), 5–13.

Wright, D. J. "Minority Students: Developmental Beginnings." In D. J. Wright (ed.), *Responding to the Needs of Today's Minority Students.* New Directions for Student Services, no. 38. San Francisco: Jossey-Bass, 1987.

*THADDEUS M. RAUSHI is a counselor at Schenectady County Community College, Schenectady, New York.*

*As the only structured service on campus that guarantees students some kind of interaction with a concerned representative of the institution, academic advising is critical for student retention and successful transfer.*

# Academic Advising, Retention, and Transfer

*Margaret C. King*

Students come to two-year colleges with a variety of goals—to take a few classes for personal enrichment or specific job training, to earn a one-year certificate, to earn a two-year degree in preparation for employment, or for continued education in a four-year college or university. Those of us working in two-year colleges have a responsibility to help students achieve those goals.

Students also come with a wide variety of backgrounds. Many are first-generation college students with little or no understanding of how colleges operate. Others are undecided about their education and career plans. Many are underprepared, needing remedial assistance in reading, writing, and mathematics before they can successfully tackle college-level courses. And there are sizable numbers of students from underrepresented populations. As Boyer (1988, p. 9) has noted, "Members of minorities who complete high school are more likely than white students to attend community colleges. These colleges enroll 55 percent of Native American college students, 43 percent of all black students, and 42 percent of all Asian students who attend institutions of higher education in America." Further, many community college students are returning adults, and almost all are commuters.

First-generation college students, racial minorities, students needing remediation, and commuting students each possess characteristics that have been linked to higher college attrition. Consequently, two-year colleges need strong support services to help students remain in the institutions and achieve their goals. Academic advising is perhaps the most critical of those services.

Academic advising is the only structured service on our campuses that guarantees students some kind of interaction with concerned representatives of the institutions. Advising can therefore be viewed as the hub of the student services wheel, providing the linkages with other support services such as career planning, counseling, financial aid, and tutoring. Advisers play a key role in helping students become integrated within the academic and social systems on campus, which in turn contributes to student growth, satisfaction, and persistence. Advisers also play a key role in providing the support, encouragement, and assistance needed for students to continue their education at four-year colleges or universities.

## Advising and Retention

Student retention is a critical concern on two-year college campuses, and with good reason. Tinto (1987, pp. 17–19) has cited a number of pertinent statistics: (1) only 29.5 percent of the entering cohort in two-year colleges will persist over a two-year period in the institutions in which they first register; (2) over an extended period, 27 percent will complete the program in the institutions in which they first enrolled; and (3) only about 46 percent of all two-year college entrants will eventually obtain either a two- or four-year degree. He has also pointed out that the rate of student departures from the higher education system is highest during the first year of college (p. 21) and is particularly high during the first six weeks of the students' first semester (p. 49).

While early research on retention identified particular student characteristics that related to attrition, such as high school grades and socioeconomic background, more recent research has focused on models of student persistence and on measures of student growth, satisfaction, and persistence within those models. Tinto (1987) has developed perhaps the best known and most tested model.

## Retention: Academic and Social Integration

Tinto's (1987) model is based on the work of Dutch anthropologist Arnold Van Gennep and of French sociologist Emile Durkheim (see Figure 2.1). Van Gennep (1960) studied the movement of individuals within society from youth to adulthood. He identified three stages of transition through which youth pass as they move to adult membership within a given society: (1) separation from past associations; (2) transition, as the person begins to interact in new ways with the new group; and (3) incorporation, as the individual becomes an established member of that group. Tinto has applied these stages to college students, noting that they are typical of the transitions that students make when they enter college and move toward membership within their new community. A student may depart the institution when he or she has difficulty negotiating those stages.

# Figure 2.1. Stages of Academic and Social Integration of College Students

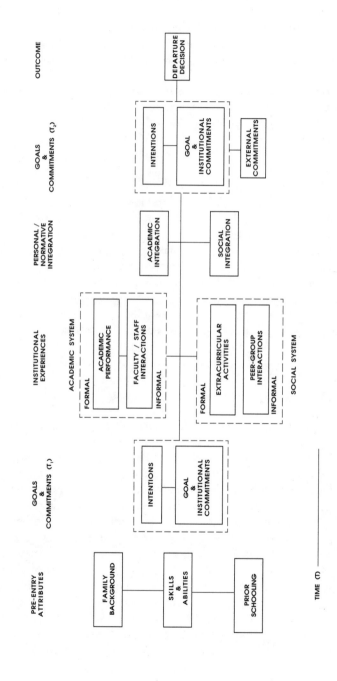

*Source:* Tinto, 1987, p. 114.

Durkheim studied suicide and theorized that one form of suicide occurs when individuals are unable to become integrated into and to establish membership within their society. That membership occurs through the process of social and intellectual integration. When this membership is not established, individuals in extreme cases withdraw from that society by committing suicide. Tinto applied that theory to higher education. He views colleges and universities as small societies, made up of distinct academic and social components. For students to establish membership within that society, they need to become integrated into the social and academic systems that exist on campus. As Tinto (1987, pp. 105–106) has explained,

> The academic system concerns itself almost entirely with the academic affairs of the college, that is, with the formal education of students. Its activities center about the classrooms and laboratories of the institution and involve various faculty and staff whose primary responsibility is to attend to the training of students. . . . The social system of the college centers about the daily life and personal needs of the various members of the institution. It is made up of those recurring sets of interactions among students, faculty and staff which take place largely outside the academic domain of the college. For students, at least, it goes on in large measure outside the formal confines of the classroom in the dormitories and hallways of the college. Its activities center on the social as well as intellectual needs of its members.

Failure to establish membership can result in student withdrawal from the institution, analogous to the withdrawal from society in Durkheim's view of suicide.

Tinto's model posits that individuals enter institutions of higher education with varying background attributes and experiences, factors over which institutions have no control. These contribute to the students' intentions, goals, and commitments to the institutions that they are attending. For example, because of their backgrounds, some students enter college with very clear education and career goals and with very strong commitments to earning their degrees. Others, especially community college students, enter college with less well established goals and commitments. Once a student enters an institution, subsequent experiences occur within the academic and social systems of the institution that involve interaction with faculty, staff, and students. If that interaction is positive and the student becomes integrated into those systems, then the student's goals and institutional commitment will be strengthened and he or she will be likely to persist at that institution. If the experiences are negative and the student fails to become integrated within the institution, the student will be more likely to withdraw.

Pascarella and Terenzini (1980) operationalized the Tinto model, determining that it had predictive validity for institutions of higher education. They measured academic and social integration through the development of five scales: (1) students' peer group interactions (for example, "The student friendships I have developed at this university have been personally satisfying"); (2) students' informal interactions with faculty (for example, "My nonclassroom interactions with faculty and staff have had a positive influence on my personal growth, values, and attitudes"); (3) students' perceptions of faculty concern for student development and teaching (for example, "Few of the faculty members I have had contact with are genuinely interested in students"); (4) students' academic and intellectual development (for example, "I am satisfied with my academic experience at this university"); and (5) students' institutional and goal commitments (for example, "It is important for me to graduate from college"). Controlling for background characteristics such as sex, academic aptitude, and parents' education, they concluded that academic and social integration contribute significantly to student persistence and noted that the frequency and quality of student-faculty informal contact were particularly important. Terenzini and Wright (1987) found that for both intellectual growth and personal growth, academic integration is more influential than social integration in the first two years of study.

While Pascarella and Terenzini specifically applied Tinto's model to four-year institutions, other studies have applied the model to two-year colleges. Pascarella and Chapman (1983) compared withdrawal from two-year commuter institutions with four-year commuter institutions and four-year residential institutions and found that in the two-year commuter sample academic integration was more important than social integration. Pascarella (1986, p. 66), in a longitudinal study of 825 students enrolled in eighty-five two-year institutions, also identified the importance of academic and social integration and concluded that "the students experience of college may have an important, unique influence on system persistence beyond that of differences in family background, secondary school experiences, individual attributes and the initial commitments with which he or she enters college. Thus it may be possible to enhance student persistence in postsecondary education through purposeful institutional policies and practices designed to enhance student social and academic integration." Halpin (1990) studied entering full-time freshmen at a small, open-door, nonresidential community college in upstate New York. Using a questionnaire similar to that used by Pascarella and Terenzini (1980), he too found that academic integration was a significant predictor of student persistence: "While little can be done to influence background characteristics or environmental circumstances of community college students, the creation of institutional mechanisms to maximize student/faculty contact is likely to result in greater levels of integration and hence persistence" (Halpin, 1990, p. 4). He also noted, moreover, that faculty-student academic contact was more influential than faculty-student social contact.

One can conclude, then, that strong developmental academic advising programs that promote student interaction with faculty and staff can greatly enhance a student's integration into the academic and social systems of the institution. That integration then contributes to student growth, satisfaction, and persistence.

## Themes of Attrition in Retention Efforts

Another way to view the role of academic advising in retention efforts is to look at the themes of attrition identified by Noel, Levitz, Saluri, and Associates (1985). Those themes, and the role that the adviser might play in each, are as follows:

*Academic boredom.* Academic boredom occurs when learning is not relevant and when students are not challenged. The advisers must provide rationales for courses to be taken in order to help students understand how those courses relate to life beyond the institution. They must also be concerned with placing students in appropriate, challenging courses as determined by the students' backgrounds and placement test scores.

*Uncertainty about major and career goals.* Noel, Levitz, Saluri, and Associates (1985, p. 121) have indicated that "uncertainty about what to study is the most frequent reason talented students give for dropping out of college." Gordon (1984, p. ix) has noted that 50 to 70 percent of entering college students will change their major at least once. Consequently, uncertainty about major and career goals is more the norm than the exception. Students in this situation are more prone to dropping out unless they get help with the career decision-making process. Depending on a student's degree of indecision and the adviser's capability with regard to career planning, the adviser can either directly assist the student with that process or refer the student to the appropriate office on campus.

*Transition and adjustment difficulties.* With respect to the earlier-cited stages of transition identified by Van Gennep, the adviser needs to be aware of the problems of transition and to be able to help students identify and articulate those problems. Only then can the adviser provide either direct assistance or appropriate referral to another resource on campus.

*Limited or unrealistic expectations of college.* Because many two-year college students are first-generation college students, they do not know what to expect. Consequently, the adviser plays a critical role in helping the student negotiate the system and develop a realistic understanding of the demands of college life.

*Academic underpreparedness.* On most two-year college campuses, underpreparedness is the norm, not the exception. Consequently, placement testing, followed by advising and appropriate course placement is critical to student success and retention. The adviser must carefully review the student's academic background and placement test results and provide appropriate interpretation before recommending courses. The adviser should also be a referral agent to the appropriate academic support services on campus.

*Incompatibility.* Creamer (1980) began his description of an advising model with the words *recruit ethically.* Advising and retention begin with the admissions process and include the provision of specific and accurate information about the institution to the prospective student.

*Relevance.* Advisers play a key role in providing for students a concrete rationale for the courses that they are required to take, helping them see a relationship between their courses and their lives and work outside the campus.

## A Population-Specific Perspective on Retention

Ramirez and Evans's (1988) study of minority students on probation is worth noting because of its implications for advising and retention. Among the eight factors identified either as characteristic of students who are not progressing satisfactorily or as characteristic of their circumstances on campus are the following:

*Inappropriate course selection and poor scheduling.* Students may ignore prerequisites and schedule classes back to back, similar to the high school format, leaving little time for support services. The adviser must explain the concept and importance of prerequisites and show students where to find information about prerequisites. They should recommend schedules that encourage involvement and provide time for students to utilize support services.

*Low use of support services.* Because they are not able to "self-assess, investigate and pursue needed support services" (Ramirez and Evans, 1988, p. 38), students frequently do not know how to negotiate the system or how to ask for help when they encounter difficulties. Advisers must provide that assistance, particularly during students' first semester, and empower students to independently make use of the colleges' resources.

*Faculty members with limited familiarity with the resources available on campus.* Faculty who have little or no familiarity with student support services on campus are unable to detect underlying problems. As Weston (this volume) discusses, adviser training is critical to effective advising.

*External factors.* The adviser needs to help students identify problems such as financial difficulties, family obligations, and job schedules and then directly or indirectly assist the students in resolving them.

*Inability to anticipate and adjust to the impact of personal life changes.*

Events such as marriage can affect a student's educational experience. The adviser needs to help students anticipate such impacts.

*Lack of a mandatory, comprehensive advising process.* High-risk students must be identified on entry and their progress monitored. An effective advising program can identify these populations and provide more intrusive advising services for them.

Although Ramirez and Evans's (1988) study was conducted at a four-year university, it is equally relevant to two-year college students and shows the importance of effective advising in enhancing the success and retention of high-risk students.

## Impact of Advising on Retention

In other research on retention, Beal and Noel (1980, pp. 44–45), reporting on a national survey conducted by the American College Testing Program and the National Center for Higher Education Management Systems, noted that "inadequate academic advising" emerged as the strongest negative factor in student retention, while "a caring attitude of faculty and staff" and "high quality of advising" emerged among the strongest positive factors. Webb (1987) identified effective academic and career advising and friendship with at least one faculty member as campus factors associated with persistence. Smith (1983), in surveying nonreturning students in a community and technical college, found that counseling and advising services were listed as the most important factors that, if effective, would have encouraged them to stay. Many other researchers have described enhanced student retention as a result of improved advising services.

Crockett (1978) described academic advising as a cornerstone of student retention, noting that when it is provided effectively, it helps students develop more mature education and career goals, strengthens the relationship between academic preparation and the world of work, and contributes to the development of a more positive attitude and better academic performance. A strong developmental academic advising program, by promoting student interaction with faculty and staff, can enhance student integration into the academic and social systems of our colleges and can help students with transition and adjustment difficulties. As Kemerer (1985, p. 8) has stated, "Virtually every study of retention has shown that a well-developed advising program is an important retention strategy. Advisors who are knowledgeable, enthusiastic, and like working with students can often make the difference between a potential dropout and a persister."

## Advising and Transfer

Just as advising plays a critical role in student retention in the two-year college, it also serves a critical role in the transfer process. Why is this important? According to Boyer (1988, pp. 5–6), two-year colleges enroll approximately 43 percent of the nation's undergraduates and 51 percent of all first-time entering freshmen. And, as noted earlier, two-year colleges enroll large percentages of minority populations. Studies have shown that these populations, which make up about 30 percent of community college enrollment, are the least likely to continue their education in a four-year college (Watkins, 1990, p. A1). As we consider issues of access and equal opportunity, this low percentage of minority student transfers has serious implications.

Although many entering two-year college students do not want or need to go on to a four-year college to attain their career goals, we need to recognize that for others transfer is appropriate and desirable. Yet, research shows that even among those students who initially plan to transfer, many do not. Watkins (1990, p. A37) has estimated that while as many as one-third of the students in two-year colleges plan to continue their education, only 15 to 25 percent actually do so.

**Obstacles to Transfer.** What are the obstacles to transfer and how do they relate to advising? Wechsler (1989) has identified seven factors:

*Academic and Articulation Barriers.* Many students find that four-year colleges either will not accept some of their credits or will accept courses as electives rather than as required courses; consequently, students have to take additional courses to complete their baccalaureate degrees. This can be discouraging. Articulation agreements may be one answer to this problem, but students need to be made aware of the agreements. Advisers need to identify, early in the process, those students who plan to transfer, ensuring that they follow the appropriate program for transfer and are aware of existing articulation agreements. Where appropriate, early referral to the campus transfer counselor or coordinator is an important step. Good academic advising is even more important in the absence of articulation agreements.

*Inadequate Support Systems.* Advisers often neglect to identify, early in the process, those students who plan to transfer. And advisers often fail to identify those qualified students who have yet to view transfer as an option and to provide them with the support and encouragement needed to explore such opportunities. This is a particularly important role for the adviser who works with minority students. Also, because support systems often do not exist on the four-year campuses, advisers need to prepare students for what they will encounter upon transferring. Sometimes the adviser or transfer counselor can also provide linkages with former students who have trans-ferred to a given institution or can help the student make connections with appropriate staff at the four-year college.

*Economic Barriers.* Frequently, the higher cost of a four-year college becomes a barrier to transfer. Advisers can help students explore options in meeting or reducing the costs and can encourage their advisees to work directly with financial aid personnel.

*Bureaucratic Barriers.* Admissions policies, deadlines, and lack of information related to transfer can be a problem. Again, by identifying advisees who are considering transfer early in the process, advisers can help them overcome these barriers.

*Geographical Barriers.* Four-year colleges may not be located in areas convenient for many two-year college students. Advisers need to help their students explore the available options, including external degree options.

*Age Impediments.* Many four-year colleges cater to the traditional age student and do not have programs and services geared to adults. Advisers can alert their adult advisees of these factors and work with them in planning how specific needs might be met.

*Racial and Ethnic Concerns.* Minority students often find that the host four-year institutions are less diverse, larger, and more impersonal than community colleges. The role of the adviser is to make students aware of these issues and help them develop plans for dealing with specific needs.

**Impact of Advising on Transfer.** Because academic advising is the only structured service on our campuses that guarantees students some kind of interaction with concerned representatives of the institutions, the adviser is in a key position to assist students with the transfer process. By identifying potential transfers early, by informing them of existing articulation agreements, by referring them to special transfer offices for assistance, and by providing the necessary support and encouragement, advisers can enhance transfer opportunities for many students. Effective performance of these tasks on a campuswide basis, however, requires a structured advising program that is well integrated with other campus support services and that provides adequate training and resources for the advisers. Through effective advising, education can become the "seamless web" that Boyer (1988, p. 36) has envisioned.

## References

Beal, P. E., and Noel, L. *What Works in Student Retention: The Report of a Joint Project of the American College Testing Program and the National Center for Higher Education Management Systems.* Iowa City, Iowa: American College Testing and the National Center for Higher Education Management Systems, 1980. 142 pp. (ED 197 635)

Boyer, E. L. *Building Communities: A Vision for a New Century.* Washington, D.C.: American Association for Community and Junior Colleges, 1988.

Creamer, D. "Educational Advising for Student Retention: An Institutional Perspective." *Community College Review,* 1980, 7 (4), 11–18.

Crockett, D. S. "Academic Advising: A Cornerstone of Student Retention." In L. Noel (ed.), *Reducing the Dropout Rate.* New Directions for Student Services, no. 3. San Francisco: Jossey-Bass, 1978.

Gordon, V. N. *The Undecided College Student: An Academic and Career Advising Challenge.* Springfield, Ill.: Thomas, 1984. 125 pp. (ED 261 639)

Halpin, R. L. "An Application of the Tinto Model to the Analysis of Freshman Persistence in a Community College." *Community College Review,* 1990, 17 (4), 22–32.

Kemerer, F. R. "The Role of Deans, Department Chairs and Faculty in Enrollment Management." *College Board Review,* 1985, 134, 4–8.

Noel, L., Levitz, R., Saluri, D., and Associates. *Increasing Student Retention: Effective Programs and Practices for Reducing the Dropout Rate.* San Francisco: Jossey-Bass, 1985.

Pascarella, E. T. "Long-Term Persistence of Two-Year College Students." *Research in Higher Education,* 1986, *24* (1), 47–71.

Pascarella, E. T., and Chapman, D. W. "A Multi-Institutional, Path Analytic Validation of Tinto's Model of College Withdrawal." *American Educational Research Journal,* 1983, *20* (1), 87–102.

Pascarella, E. T., and Terenzini, P. T. "Predicting Freshman Persistence and Voluntary Dropout Decisions from a Theoretical Model." *Journal of Higher Education,* 1980, *51* (1), 60–75.

Ramirez, J. D., and Evans, R. "Solving the Probation Puzzle—a Student Affirmative Action Program." *NACADA Journal,* 1988, *8* (2), 34–45.

Smith, A. D. "Stated Reasons for Withdrawal and Degrees of Satisfaction Among Student Persisters and Non-Persisters." *NACADA Journal,* 1983, *3* (1), 73–84.

Terenzini, P. T., and Wright, T. M. "Influences on Students' Academic Growth During Four Years of College." *Research in Higher Education,* 1987, *26* (2), 161–179.

Tinto, V. *Leaving College: Rethinking the Causes and Cures of Student Attrition.* Chicago: University of Chicago Press, 1987. 246 pp. (ED 283 416)

Van Gennep, A. *The Rites of Passage.* (M. Vizedon and G. Caffee, trans.) Chicago: University of Chicago Press, 1960.

Watkins, B. T. "Two-Year Institutions Under Pressure to Ease Transfers." *Chronicle of Higher Education,* 1990, *36* (21), A1, A37–A38.

Webb, E. M. "Retention and Excellence Through Student Involvement: A Leadership Role for Student Affairs." *NASPA Journal,* 1987, *24* (4), 6–11.

Wechsler, H. *The Transfer Challenge: Removing Barriers, Maintaining Commitment.* Washington, D.C.: Association of American Colleges, 1989. 76 pp. (ED 317 127)

MARGARET C. KING *is assistant dean for student development at Schenectady County Community College, Schenectady, New York. She currently serves as president of the National Academic Advising Association (1991–1993).*

*The American College Testing Program's fourth national survey, a source of data on the status of academic advising, reflects the state of the art of advising in community colleges.*

# The Organization and Effectiveness of Academic Advising in Community Colleges

*Wesley R. Habley*

The contribution of effective academic advising to student success is, by now, obvious to most faculty and administrators in community colleges. These individuals recognize that students who formulate sound education and career plans based on their values, interests, and abilities have an increased chance for academic success, satisfaction, and persistence. Academic advising remains the most significant mechanism available on most community college campuses for aiding and abetting this important process. Substantive advising services are a prerequisite to the successful transition of students into the community college environment as well as to their persistence to education goal attainment. This chapter highlights selected results from community colleges that participated in the American College Testing (ACT) Program's fourth national survey on the status of academic advising (Habley, 1993). Included in this chapter are preliminary survey results on organizational models, coordination and reporting lines, institutional policy statements, adviser training, adviser evaluation, recognition and reward, program goals, and program effectiveness.

## Institutional Sample of the Fourth ACT Survey

The data from the fourth ACT survey reflect a sample of institutions drawn from a total population of 932 public two-year colleges. The sample included 232 institutions, of which respondents at 159 institutions (68.5 percent) returned usable surveys. As a result of the sampling technique and the response rate, it can be assumed that the sample is nationally representative of community colleges with a sampling error level of less than 5 percent. Each survey was mailed to the director or coordinator of academic advising with a request that the survey be completed by the person most knowledgeable about the institution's advising program. As a result, survey responses represent the views of those individuals. The titles of the most common community college respondents were director of counseling (21 percent), director or coordinator of advising (15 percent), vice president or dean of academic affairs (15 percent), and vice president or dean of student affairs (10 percent). Twenty-seven percent of the respondents fell in the survey category "other." Although the survey focused on advising practices in both two-year and four-year public and private institutions, only the results of two-year public institutions are reported in this chapter.

### Organizational Models and Program Coordination

Habley (1983) proposed the existence of seven basic organizational models of advising programs and Habley and McCauley (1987) studied the prevalence of these models:

*Faculty only:* All students are assigned to instructional faculty members for advising.

*Supplementary:* All students are assigned to instructional faculty members for advising. There is an advising office that provides general academic information and referral for students, but all advising transactions must be approved by the student's faculty adviser.

*Split:* There is an advising office that advises a specific group of students (for example, undecided, underprepared, nontraditional). Advising in the advising office occurs for a specified period of time or until a specific set of requirements have been completed. All other students are assigned to instructional units or faculty for advising.

*Dual:* Each student has two advisers. A member of the instructional faculty advises the student on matters related to the major. An adviser in an advising office advises the student on general requirements, procedures, and policies.

*Total intake:* Staff in an administrative unit are responsible for advising all students for a specified period of time or until specific requirements have been met. After meeting those requirements, each student is assigned to a member of the instructional faculty for advising.

*Satellite:* Each school, college, or division within the institution has established a unit that is responsible for advising students within that unit.

*Self-contained:* Advising for all students from point of first enrollment to point of departure is done by staff in a centralized advising unit.

More complete descriptions of the models are provided by King (this volume, Chapter Four) as well as by Habley (1983, 1988) and Habley and McCauley (1987).

The percentage of respondents from two-year public institutions utilizing each of the institutional models was as follows: self-contained (30 percent), faculty only (27 percent), split (20 percent), dual (8 percent), supplementary (6 percent), total intake (6 percent), and satellite (1 percent). Although it may seem a paradox that the most centralized (self-contained) and the most decentralized (faculty-only) models are the two most utilized models in the two-year public college, it is reasonable to assume that there are precedents in the utilization of those models. The self-contained and the faculty-only models may simply be adaptations of guidance models existing in other educational settings: The self-contained is more directly related to a high school guidance model where academic and personal counseling are combined, and the faculty-only model relates to the predominant model employed in four-year institutions. The deployment of the split model in one-fifth of the institutions may reflect the colleges' responsiveness to special populations of students (for example, underprepared, nontraditional, and undecided). The utilization of either the supplementary model or the dual model may indicate the institution's belief in a faculty advising system tempered by the reality that faculty may not always be able or available to meet the needs of the diverse set of student constituencies served by the community college.

As intimated by the distribution of advising models, the titles of the individuals responsible for coordinating advising also varied widely across the institutions. Although the most common title was director of counseling (24 percent), advising coordination was also attributed to the director or coordinator of academic advising (17 percent), vice president or dean of academic affairs (12 percent), and vice president or dean of student affairs (11 percent). Coordination in the remaining community colleges was attributed to the assistant vice president or dean of student affairs (4 percent), assistant vice president or dean of academic affairs (2 percent), college dean or department chair (6 percent), and a relatively large "other" category (18 percent). Finally, it is important to report that only two (1 percent) of the community colleges reported that no one was responsible for the coordination of academic advising.

An obvious offshoot of both the organizational models and the titles of those who coordinate and direct advising services in the community college is the time that the individuals devote to the coordination of these activities. In the present survey, nearly two-thirds (66 percent) of those who coordinated campus advising reported that they spent less than one-quarter of their time, 16 percent reported spending one-half of their time, and 11 percent reported spending three-quarters of their time. Finally, only 7 percent engaged in the coordination of the advising system as a full-time role.

## Institutional Policy Statement on Academic Advising

If advising is considered an important function in the community college, then it is imperative that a comprehensive institutional policy statement be developed to guide the advising activities. A goal of the ACT survey was to ascertain the existence of advising policies and to gain some understanding of the foci of such policy statements. Regarding the existence of institutional advising policy statements, only 60 percent (ninety-five institutions) indicated that such a statement existed, while the remaining 40 percent (sixty-four institutions) reported that no statement existed. Table 3.1 provides a breakdown of the elements detailed in the existing policy statements.

Table 3.1 indicates that among the institutions with policy statements, the topics of those statements were general in nature: philosophy, goals, adviser responsibilities, and delivery strategies. Only limited attention was given to the selection, training, evaluation, and recognition and reward for advisers, factors that are critical to the success of an advising program.

## Adviser Training

Data gathered on the training of advisers in community colleges, both in advising offices and in academic departments or divisions, concern the existence of training programs, topics included, and formats employed. In the area of mandated training, only 46 percent of respondents indicated that required faculty adviser training existed in all departments or divisions, and 29 percent of the institutions indicated that faculty adviser training was mandated in none of their departments or divisions. The remaining community colleges (25 percent) had mandatory faculty adviser training in some departments or divisions. And although it would seem safe to assume that advising office advisers participate in extensive preservice and in-service training, such an assumption was not completely borne out by these national

### Table 3.1. Elements Detailed in Respondents' Policy Statements on Academic Advising

| Elements | Percentage of Institutions |
|---|---|
| Philosophy | 78 |
| Goals | 80 |
| Adviser responsibilities | 74 |
| Delivery strategies | 59 |
| Advisee responsibilities | 49 |
| Adviser selection | 30 |
| Adviser training | 30 |
| Adviser evaluation | 25 |
| Adviser recognition and reward | 3 |

Note: N = 159 institutions.

Source: Habley, 1993.

survey data, where 35 percent of the institutions responded by stating that training either did not exist or was not mandated for staff in the advising office.

In reviewing the topics included in training programs for faculty advisers, survey data were grouped into three content areas: *key concepts* in advising (things that advisers should understand), *information needs* (things that advisers should know), and *relationship skills* (things that advisers should demonstrate). In Table 3.2, the topics are grouped by the three content areas with the percentage (in parentheses) of institutions reporting coverage of each topic for faculty advisers in all academic departments or divisions.

Two observations can be made in relationship to these data. First, the data include only those institutions indicating that training programs for faculty advisers did indeed exist on their campuses. Second, although each of the three topical areas is important to the effectiveness of individual advisers, training in concepts and information was most prominent, while relationship skills received limited attention.

Table 3.3 uses the same topical groupings to look at the training that took place in community college advising offices. As with training in the academic departments, the heaviest training emphasis in advising offices was in the area of information needs, with some focus also in the conceptual area. Training in relationship skills apparently was more prevalent in advising office training than it was in faculty adviser training.

The final component of the community college adviser training effort reviewed in the national survey involved the format for training programs both in advising offices and in academic departments or divisions. Table 3.4 reports the percentage distribution of institutions employing particular formats for adviser training in advising offices and in academic departments. The "All" column reports the percentages of institutions at which the

### Table 3.2. Topics Included in Community College Faculty Adviser Training

| Key Concepts | Information Needs | Relationship Skills |
|---|---|---|
| Importance of advising (55) | Regulations, policies, and procedures (63) | Counseling skills (26) |
| Definition of advising (44) | Campus referral sources (50) | Interviewing skills (20) |
| | Uses of information sources (53) | Decision-making skills (15) |
| | Career and employment information (18) | |

*Note:* N = 159 institutions; parenthetical figures are the percentages of respondent institutions reporting coverage of the topics for faculty advisers in all academic departments or divisions.

*Source:* Habley, 1993.

particular format was utilized for all departments, while the "None" column reports the percentage of institutions at which a particular training format was employed in none of the departments.

Three messages can be gleaned from Table 3.4. First, advising office training in the sample institutions was apparently highly individualized and spaced throughout the academic year. Second, faculty adviser training, if it existed at all, was not consistently utilized within the institutions. Finally, the predominant format for faculty adviser training occurred once a year (the faculty meeting before classes started) and was limited to one day or less.

### Program and Adviser Evaluation

In order to gain some measure of the quality of academic advising in the community college, it is necessary to design and implement evaluation

#### Table 3.3. Topics Included in Community College Advising Office Training

| Key Concepts | Information Needs | Relationship Skills |
|---|---|---|
| Importance of advising (67) | Regulations, policies and procedures (96) | Counseling skills (49) |
| Definition of advising (58) | Campus referral sources (82) | Interviewing skills (35) |
| | Uses of information sources (81) | Decision-making skills (29) |
| | Career and employment information (55) | |

Note: N = 159 institutions; parenthetical figures are the percentages of respondent institutions reporting coverage of the topics for staff in college advising offices.

Source: Habley, 1993.

#### Table 3.4. Percentage Distribution of Community College Adviser Training Formats

| Format | Advising Offices | Departments All | Departments None |
|---|---|---|---|
| Single workshop of one day or less | 96 | 32 | 17 |
| Series of short workshops throughout the year | 49 | 20 | 23 |
| Single workshop longer than a day | 82 | 4 | 30 |
| Method varied by adviser | 35 | 11 | 19 |
| Other | 55 | 9 | 7 |

Note: N = 159 institutions.

Source: Habley, 1993.

strategies at both the program and individual adviser levels. Table 3.5 characterizes program evaluation efforts in community colleges for both the overall advising system and for advising offices on campuses that reported the existence of such offices. Table 3.5 suggests that program evaluation both in advising offices and for campuswide advising systems is not a universally accepted concept, and, unfortunately, neither is the evaluation of individual advisers.

Table 3.6 reports the scope of methods used to evaluate faculty advisers. Of significance in Table 3.6 is the apparent lack of a consistent institutional approach to the evaluation of an individual faculty advising effort. Without a definitive institutional policy on evaluation, academic departments appear to be at liberty to decide both whether to evaluate advising activity and, if they choose to evaluate, which methods to employ.

The scope of adviser evaluation in community college advising offices was no more encompassing than the evaluation of faculty advisers. Just under 28 percent of the community colleges with advising offices reported that no formal methods were employed in the evaluation of advisers. For those offices that reported formal evaluation, just over 75 percent employed a performance review by the office supervisor as a component of evaluation, while just under 50 percent reported student evaluation and less than 33 percent reported self-evaluation as components of the adviser evaluation system.

### Table 3.5.  Percentages of Institutions
### Reporting Regular Program Evaluation

| Target | Yes | No |
|---|---|---|
| Advising office | 54 | 46 |
| Advising system | 50 | 50 |

Note: N = 159 institutions.

Source: Habley, 1993.

### Table 3.6.  Percentage Distribution of Community
### College Methods for Evaluating Faculty Advisers

| Method | All Departments | No Departments |
|---|---|---|
| Student evaluation | 24 | 37 |
| Self-evaluation | 19 | 32 |
| Supervisory performance review | 28 | 26 |

Note: N = 159 institutions.

Source: Habley, 1993.

## Recognition and Reward for Advising

Although the fourth ACT survey did not attempt to gather data on recognition and reward for advisers in community college advising offices, data were gathered on the existence of a recognition and reward system for faculty advisers. These data, to say the least, paint a bleak picture. Data on the methods of recognition and reward in the community colleges that rewarded faculty advisers show that very few institutions consistently applied a reward strategy for *all* of their departments, leaving each department or division at liberty to include (or exclude) advising from the reward considerations for faculty.

Several possible approaches to faculty adviser recognition and reward, together with the percentages of community colleges that employed those approaches in *all* departments, are as follows: released time from instruction (5 percent), released time from committee work (0 percent), released time from research expectation (1 percent), salary increments for time spent in advising (5 percent), major consideration in promotion and tenure (5 percent), minor consideration in promotion and tenure (9 percent), and awards for excellence in advising (1 percent). These findings on community college reward and recognition for faculty advising support the statement that there is little institutional recognition for serving in the role of faculty adviser.

## Advising Program Goals

In the national survey section on advising goals, community college respondents were asked to rate their advising programs' effectiveness on eight goals that were first endorsed by the National Academic Advising Association (NACADA) and later served as the basis for the guidelines of the Council for the Advancement of Standards for Student Services and Development Programs (1986). Respondents were asked to rate, on the scale below, the extent to which advising services were delivered or designed to successfully achieve the goals for *most* students.

1. Does not apply; no services have been implemented to address this goal
2. Achievement not very satisfactory
3. Achievement somewhat satisfactory
4. Achievement satisfactory
5. Achievement very satisfactory

The goals, with mean ratings (in parentheses), were as follows: providing accurate information about institutional policies, procedures, resources, and programs (4.0); providing information about students to the institution, colleges, academic departments, or combination thereof (3.4); making referrals to other institutional or community support services (3.6); assisting students in developing education plans consistent with life goals and objectives (alternative courses of action, alternate career considerations, and selection of courses) (3.5); assisting students in evaluation or reevaluation of progress toward established goals and education plans (3.5); assisting students in their consideration of life goals by relating interests, skills, abilities, and values to careers, the world of work, and the nature and purpose of higher education (3.1); assisting students in self-understanding and self-acceptance (value clarification, understanding abilities, interests, and limitations) (2.8); and assisting students in developing decision-making skills (2.7). Although community college survey respondents appeared to be reasonably positive about their advising programs' ability to provide traditional advising services such as accurate information, referral, and review of academic progress, they were less satisfied with program performance in life planning, student self-understanding, and the development of decision-making skills.

## Current Effectiveness and Recent Progress in Campus Advising Systems

Survey respondents were also asked to consider both the current effectiveness of their campus advising programs and the progress made during the previous five years. Based on the rating scale of 1 (very ineffective) to 5 (very effective) for current effectiveness and the scale of 1 (much less effective) to 5 (much more effective) to rate recent progress, the community college mean scores are reported in Table 3.7.

The data in Table 3.7 suggest that there is both bad and good news. The bad news is that community college respondents rated four variables below the midpoint (3.00) on the effectiveness scale, suggesting that they believed that accountability, training, evaluation, and recognition and reward were more ineffective than effective. The good news warrants caution. Although there was progress on some of the effectiveness variables, there appeared to be dissatisfaction with progress in other areas. Seven variables were rated above the midpoint (3.00) on the progress scale, with the most significant progress being cited in advisee information (3.8) and meeting student needs (3.7).

## Commentary

Although it is conceded by most community college faculty and administrators that academic advising is a critical service to students, conversion of that belief into concrete action and systematic program planning appears to be far from the norm. Certainly, if one were to characterize the effectiveness of any function, such a description would include establishing clear guidelines

Table 3.7.  Mean Scores on Scales Rating Current
Effectiveness and Recent Progress of Advising Programs

| Variable | Effectiveness | Progress |
|---|---|---|
| Advisee information: providing advisers with timely and accurate information on their advisees | 3.6 | 3.8 |
| Meeting student needs: providing for the advising needs of students | 3.4 | 3.7 |
| Adviser traits: providing advisers who are willing to participate in advising, have at least the basic skills necessary for advising, and have the time necessary to do an effective job of advising | 3.6 | 3.5 |
| Campuswide communication: providing for communication among and between deans, department heads, advisers, and the coordinator of advising (if such a position exists) | 3.5 | 3.5 |
| Program economy: meeting students' needs when combined with the expenditure of human and fiscal resources | 3.4 | 3.4 |
| Adviser selection: identifying and selecting individuals to participate in advising | 3.4 | 3.3 |
| Campuswide coordination: providing appropriate levels of coordination, direction, and supervision | 3.2 | 3.3 |
| Accountability: providing adviser accountability both to a higher level of authority and to advisees | 2.8 | 2.9 |
| Training: implementing a training program for advisers | 2.8 | 2.9 |
| Evaluation: systematically evaluating both the advising program and advisers | 2.8 | 2.8 |
| Recognition and reward: recognizing and rewarding quality advising | 2.1 | 2.2 |

Note: Effectiveness scale ranged from 1 (very ineffective) to 5 (very effective), progress scale ranged from 1 (much less effective) to 5 (much more effective).

Source: Habley, 1993.

for the function, ensuring that all aspects of the function are coordinated, providing adequate training for the individuals engaged in the function, evaluating both the success of the function and the performance of those who engage in it, and rewarding those whose performance is exemplary. Failure to consider any one of these five variables will cause significant weakness (if not breakage) in the effectiveness chain. When one applies these activities to the function of academic advising in the community college, the results are not positive.

Following is a series of qualitative statements taken from the Council for the Advancement of Standards for Student Services and Development Programs (1986) and from Winston and others (1984). Each of the statements is followed by a recapitulation of the status of that particular activity in community college academic advising programs based on the ACT survey data (Habley, 1993).

First, the design of the academic advising program must be compatible with the institutional organizational structure and student needs (Council for the Advancement of Standards for Student Services and Development Programs, 1986, p. 11). There is great diversity in the organizational models for delivering academic advising in community colleges. It is hoped, although it is not verified by survey data, that the diversity of organizational models is based on institutional structure and student needs.

Second, a specific individual must be designated by the institution to direct or coordinate the academic advising program (Council for the Advancement of Standards for Student Services and Development Programs, 1986, p. 11). Although only 1 percent of the institutions in the ACT survey reported that no one was charged with the responsibility of directing and coordinating academic advising, nearly 70 percent of the individuals who coordinated advising spent one-quarter time or less in that activity. In rating the effectiveness of campuswide program coordination, the mean for all community colleges was 3.2, a shade above the midpoint on the 5-point effectiveness scale.

Third, the institution must have a clear written statement of philosophy pertaining to academic advising that includes program goals and sets forth expectations of advisers and advisees (Council for the Advancement of Standards for Student Services and Development Programs, 1986, p. 11). Only about 60 percent of the institutions in the ACT survey had an institutional policy statement.

Fourth, academic advising should be offered only by personnel who have received systematic skills training (Winston and others, 1984, p. 24). Only 29 percent of community colleges reported that training of faculty advisers was mandated in none of their departments. Existing faculty adviser training focused primarily on the information aspects of advising, and such training usually took place in a single annual workshop of one day or less. In rating the effectiveness of adviser training, the mean for all of the community colleges in the sample was 2.8, below the midpoint of the 5-point effectiveness scale.

Fifth, there must be systematic and regular research on and evaluation of the overall academic advising program (Council for the Advancement of Standards for Student Services and Development Programs, 1986, p. 7). Only 50 percent of community colleges reported systematic evaluation of their advising programs. Only 54 percent of community colleges reported systematic evaluation of their advising offices.

Sixth, academic advising should be offered only by personnel whose performance is systematically evaluated (Winston and others, 1984, p. 24). At best, less than 50 percent of the community colleges reported systematic evaluation of their faculty advisers, and 28 percent of the community colleges reported that there was no formal evaluation for staff in advising offices. In rating the effectiveness of evaluation of advising, the mean for all institutions was 2.8, below the midpoint on the 5-point effectiveness scale.

Seventh, academic advising should be offered only by personnel who are rewarded for skillful performance (Winston and others, 1984, p. 24). The predominant method for rewarding advisers was through a minor consideration in promotion and tenure decisions, yet only 9 percent of the institutions systematically employed that method in all departments. In rating the effectiveness of adviser recognition and reward, the mean for all institutions was 2.1, far below midpoint on the 5-point effectiveness scale.

Even though the results of the national survey indicate a need for significant improvement in academic advising in community colleges, there are two major positive facets of the data. First, the mean is a reflection of central tendency. It was calculated from the respondents at 159 community colleges and included ratings from both institutions that were struggling with advising as well as institutions that had exemplary academic advising programs. For additional evidence of exemplary programs, one need only attend a regional or national meeting of NACADA or review the descriptions of community college advising systems that have won acclaim through the ACT/NACADA Awards Program (ACT Program and NACADA, 1984).

The second positive facet of the national survey data concerns program improvement. In all but one of the eleven improvement categories, as mentioned earlier, the community college respondents believed that they were more effective at the time of the survey than they were five years earlier. In fact, the overall mean for improvements in all eleven effectiveness areas was 3.2, above the midpoint of the 5-point improvement scale.

Clearly, the trend lines for various aspects of community college academic advising are in the right direction. And even though the overall current status of advising programs in community colleges is not exemplary, a continued focus on organization, coordination, training, evaluation, and reward should lead to major improvements in the years ahead.

## References

American College Testing Program and National Academic Advising Association. *The Award Winners: ACT/NACADA National Recognition Program for Academic Advising.* Iowa City, Iowa: American College Testing and National Academic Advising Association, 1984. 84 pp. (ED 256 189)

Council for the Advancement of Standards for Student Services and Development Programs. *CAS Standards and Guidelines for Student Services and Development Programs.* Iowa City, Iowa: American College Testing, 1986. 92 pp. (ED 303 757)

Habley, W. R. "Organizational Structures for Academic Advising: Models and Implications." *Journal of College Student Personnel*, 1983, 24 (6), 535–540.

Habley, W. R. (ed.). *The Status and Future of Academic Advising: Problems and Promise.* Iowa City, Iowa: American College Testing, 1988.

Habley, W. R. *Fulfilling the Promise?* Iowa City, Iowa: American College Testing, 1993.

Habley, W. R., and McCauley, M. E. "The Relationship Between Institutional Characteristics and the Organization of Advising Services." *NACADA Journal,* 1987, 7 (1), 27–39.

Winston, R. B., Jr., and others. *Developmental Academic Advising: Addressing Students' Educational, Career, and Personal Needs.* San Francisco: Jossey-Bass, 1984.

WESLEY R. HABLEY *is director of Assessment Program Services for the American College Testing Program, Iowa City, Iowa. He is past president of the National Academic Advising Association.*

*Seven organizational models of academic advising utilize a variety of delivery systems to provide advising services.*

# Advising Models and Delivery Systems

*Margaret C. King*

For many years, little attention was paid to organizational models of academic advising. This was largely due to two factors: (1) the belief that because of the uniqueness of each institution, transferability of organizational models was limited and (2) the blurring of the distinction between organizational models and delivery systems. However, research by Habley (1983) and the American College Testing (ACT) Program's third and fourth national surveys on academic advising (see Habley, 1988, 1993) have shown that organizational patterns do exist and do have interinstitutional applicability.

The way in which advising services are organized and delivered on any given campus is largely influenced by four key factors: the mission of the institution, the nature of the student population, the role of the faculty, and the programs, policies, and procedures of the institution. To have an effective system, each factor must be considered as an institution develops or redesigns academic advising services.

Several components of the institutional mission include control (whether or not the institution is public, private, or proprietary), selectivity (open door or highly selective), and the nature of the program offerings (liberal arts versus vocational-technical). Advising services may need to be organized differently at a public, two-year vocational-technical institution than they would at a private, two-year liberal arts institution.

Student characteristics also impact the organization of advising services. An institution whose students are predominantly underprepared, undecided, socioeconomically diverse, first generation, nontraditional, and commuter needs a more centralized and intrusive advising system than an institution whose students fall at the other end of the spectrum.

As Habley (this volume) discusses, faculty have a role in advising

47

services. The question of the extent of that role depends on many factors, including the faculty members' interest in advising, awareness of existing problems related to advising on the campus, and willingness to develop the skills needed to address those problems. Their role is also influenced by the priority that the administration places on advising, the extent to which effective advising is evaluated, recognized, and rewarded, and any faculty contracts or collective bargaining agreements that exist.

The fourth key factor that influences the organization and delivery of advising services deals with the complexity of institutional programs, policies, and procedures. The sequencing of courses, the complexity of graduation requirements, the scope of the general education requirement, and the degree to which the adviser must approve of a variety of academic transactions all affect the advising services. The more complexity that exists, the greater the need for skilled advisers to work within a highly structured advising system.

Three additional factors to be considered are budget, facilities, and the college's organizational structure. If there is little money, an institution may be forced to rely on existing personnel to provide the service. The availability of space to house a centralized advising service affects decisions to move in that direction. Organizational structure, dictating which office has the ultimate responsibility for advising services, also affects how those services can be organized and delivered.

## Organizational Models

Habley and McCauley (1987) made the first attempt to verify the existence of seven organizational models of advising. That research was expanded in the ACT Program's third and fourth national surveys on academic advising, described in detail in Habley (1988, 1993). Descriptions of those seven models follow.

**Faculty Only.** In this model, each student is assigned to a specific faculty member for advising, generally someone in the student's program of study. Undecided students may be assigned to faculty at large, to liberal arts faculty, to faculty who volunteer to advise them, or to faculty with lighter advising loads. This is the predominant model in private two-year colleges and is the only model in which the designation of faculty refers to both the organizational model and the delivery system. While there may be an overall advising coordinator, the supervision of advisers is generally decentralized in the academic subunits.

**Supplementary.** The supplementary advising model also uses faculty as advisers for all students in the institution. However, there is also an advising office that serves as an information clearinghouse and referral resource, but it has no original jurisdiction for approving advising transactions. The office may have a coordinator and may provide resources, implement adviser training, and develop, maintain, and update information systems. Supervision of faculty advisers occurs in the academic subunits.

**Split.** In this model, the initial advising of students is split between faculty members in academic subunits and the staff of an advising office. The advising office has original jurisdiction for advising a specific group of students (for example, undecided or underprepared students, or athletes); however, once specific conditions have been met, such as declaring their majors, students are then assigned to advisers in their respective academic subunits. The advising office has a coordinator or director and may have campuswide coordinating responsibility. The office may also serve as a referral resource for students assigned to advisers in the academic subunits.

**Dual.** In the dual advising model, students have two advisers. Faculty members provide advising related to the students' programs of study, while advisers in an advising office provide advising related to institutional academic policies and registration procedures. The advising office also generally advises undecided students and typically has a coordinator with campuswide coordinating responsibilities.

**Total Intake.** In this model, all initial advising of students is done by advisers in the advising office until a set of institutionally predetermined conditions have been met. Those conditions might consist of completion of the first semester, or completion of a specific number of credits. A director or dean of the advising office may have responsibility for campuswide coordination of advising. In four-year colleges, the advising office may also be responsible for the development of curriculum, the administration of instruction, the development and enforcement of academic policies, or a combination of these activities.

**Satellite.** In the satellite model, advising offices are maintained and controlled within the academic subunits. Satellite advising offices provide advising for all students whose majors are within a particular college or school. Undecided students are generally advised in a separate satellite office that has responsibility for overall campus coordination of advising and for providing support to all advisers.

**Self-Contained.** In this model, all advising takes place in a centralized unit. That unit is administered by a dean or director who has responsibility for all advising functions on the campus. In the ACT research, this was the predominant model used at public two-year colleges.

## Advising Delivery Systems

With the exception of the faculty-only model, organizational models of advising may utilize a variety of delivery systems. The most common of these are faculty advisers, professional (full-time) advisers, counselors, peer advisers, and paraprofessional advisers. In addition, many institutions enhance their primary delivery system through computer-assisted advising, a freshman seminar course, or both. The remainder of this chapter describes each of the delivery systems and discusses some of the strengths and weaknesses of each in regard to the following criteria: (1) accessibility and availability of the adviser to students, (2) priority placed on advising by the adviser, (3) adviser's knowledge of the major field of study, (4) adviser's knowledge of student development theory, (5) training required, (6) cost, and (7) credibility with faculty and staff.

**Faculty Advisers.** Full-time teaching faculty continue to be the primary group providing advising services for students. The accessibility and availability of faculty advisers has frequently been a concern of students, which is not surprising. For faculty, advising must compete with other priorities such as teaching, course and curriculum development, and committee work, all of which generally hold a much higher priority when it comes to institutional recognition and reward (Teague and Grites, 1980). In addition, the advising loads of faculty are frequently high. Consequently, it is not surprising that the ACT survey results (see Habley, 1988, 1993) show that the time faculty spend in advising is between 1 and 5 percent and that most faculty have contact with their advisees only two times or less per academic term. Accessibility and availability is much less of an issue in institutions where faculty advisers are selected and advise voluntarily, are provided released time to advise, and are given recognition for quality advising.

A major strength of faculty advisers is their knowledge of advising issues related to their respective disciplines. Faculty advisers generally can provide detailed information about courses and programs in their departments and the rationale for course and program requirements, and they are knowledgeable about educational and career opportunities related to their fields.

Lack of knowledge of student development theory, knowledge that is important for effective academic advising, is a weakness of faculty advisers. Consequently, they may be of less help working with undecided students or with students dealing with personal concerns than are full-time advisers or counselors. Given that quality advising is more than selecting and scheduling courses, the need for adviser training is particularly strong for faculty advisers.

Faculty advisers score high on the final two criteria—cost and credibility with faculty and staff. In institutions where advising is viewed as part of the teaching function and all faculty are required to advise, there is no additional monetary cost. And because of their rank as faculty, the credibility of faculty advisers with other faculty and staff is generally high.

One additional strength of a faculty advising delivery system that merits recognition is the demonstrated positive impact of informal student-faculty interaction on student growth, satisfaction, and persistence (Terenzini and Pascarella, 1980). A strong faculty advising program is one way of promoting such interaction.

In summary, if faculty are selected to deliver advising services, only those faculty who are interested in and capable of providing effective advising for students should be selected. Ideally, these faculty should be given released time to advise, should receive ongoing training, and should receive appropriate recognition and reward for services performed well.

**Professional Full-Time Advisers.** The second most common delivery system is the use of professional advisers, whose role focuses primarily on providing academic and support services for students. Professional advisers are generally housed in a central location, spend a full day in their offices, and devote the majority of their time to providing academic advising to students. Because they are usually hired on the basis of their interest in and ability to work with students in an advising capacity, advising is their priority. Provided they have reasonable advising loads, they are easily accessible and have more opportunity to be proactive with their advisees, initiating regular contact and follow-up, than is characteristic of other delivery systems.

While professional advisers may not possess the in-depth knowledge of courses, programs, and educational and career opportunities in a given discipline that is available from faculty advisers, they are generally more knowledgeable about the broad range of institutional programs, policies, and procedures. Consequently, they can be particularly effective with undecided students or those exploring other program options. They are also generally program-neutral and are therefore less likely to try to influence students to select particular programs or courses.

Another strength of professional advisers is knowledge of student development theory gained through their education and training. They can be particularly effective in working with advisees who are dealing with issues related to personal and career development. They are also generally knowledgeable about other services available to students, both on and off the campus, and are likely to possess refined referral skills. Consequently, when advisees need assistance beyond the adviser's capabilities, the adviser can serve as an effective referral agent for the students.

The training needs of professional advisers may be high initially, but less pressing over time. If their backgrounds are in counseling and student development, initial training focusing on information skills would be the priority, with an update needed as new courses, programs, policies, and procedures are introduced. Because the professional adviser is working with advising issues daily, formal ongoing training may be less important than for faculty.

The direct cost of using professional advisers is high, since the institution must hire special staff to perform the advising function as opposed to utilizing existing faculty. In addition, because many professional advisers do not hold faculty rank, they may not enjoy the same respect or credibility accorded to faculty.

In summary, professional advisers can be very beneficial to a comprehensive advising delivery system. However, priority must be placed on thorough initial training, a reasonable advising load, and ongoing interaction with faculty.

**Counselors.** Counselors frequently provide advising services on two-year college campuses. The strengths and weaknesses of using counselors to deliver advising services are similar to those associated with professional advisers. One exception may be in the priority placed on advising. Many times professional counselors are more interested in providing psychological and career counseling services and may view advising as less important (Crockett, 1985); consequently, advising may be given a low priority among the variety of tasks that counselors perform.

**Peer Advisers.** Peer advisers are used much more widely in advising delivery systems on four-year than on two-year college campuses, although the gap appears to be narrowing. Peer advisers have been rated as effective as faculty advisers in terms of both provision of information and the student's personal satisfaction with the adviser. Further, these advisers have been rated higher than faculty on interpersonal dimensions of the advising relationship. Peer advisers are also accepted more readily by students and may contribute to significantly lower attrition rates (Habley, 1979).

Peer advisers rate highly in terms of accessibility and availability to students, since their hours are flexible and they can work in a variety of locations. While advising is generally a priority for the peer adviser, there may be difficulty in balancing the advising and the student role. Peer advisers may also lack objectivity regarding professors and courses.

Peer advisers generally do not have the knowledge of courses and programs attributed to faculty and professional advisers, or knowledge of student development theory. Consequently, for a peer advising program to be successful, careful selection, training, and ongoing supervision are critical.

Lower cost is an obvious advantage of a peer advising program, as salaries are generally low. Peer advisers also free up professional advisers to do more in-depth advising. They can also increase student use of advising services as students feel more comfortable with other students than with professionals. On the negative side, an effective peer advising program requires significant professional staff time for training, supervision, and evaluation. Also, there is a lack of continuity and sometimes accountability because of graduation.

In summary, for a peer advising program to be effective, special attention must be given to adviser selection, training, supervision, and evaluation. When that attention is given, peer advisers can be a very valuable supplement to an advising delivery system.

**Paraprofessional Advisers.** Paraprofessionals are not students but are generally people with at least an associate degree who have an interest in working with students. In one community college model (King, 1979), paraprofessionals included retired persons, homemakers, faculty spouses, and individuals employed in different occupations during the daytime. Alumni have also been effectively used in this capacity (Kerr, 1983).

The advantages and disadvantages of a paraprofessional advising system are similar to those of a peer advising system. Paraprofessionals are accessible, economical, enthusiastic, and committed, and their use frees up the professional adviser or counselor for more in-depth advising with students who require such extra service. In addition, advising is their priority, and generally there is continuity from year to year. However, careful selection, training, and supervision remain critical for an effective system. Paraprofessionals, like peers, are most effective when used in conjunction with a faculty or professional advising delivery system rather than as the sole delivery method.

**An Ideal System?** Is there an ideal advising model and delivery system for community colleges? In my opinion the answer is yes.

The ideal model is the total-intake format in which there is a centralized advising office with a full-time director and staffed by full-time advisers or counselors and part-time faculty and paraprofessionals or peers. These advisers would be carefully selected, receive systematic skills training, have advising as a specific responsibility, and would be evaluated and receive appropriate recognition and reward for effective advising.

This office would provide, at a minimum, all initial advising for students. Ideally, advising through that office would continue throughout the student's first year, at which time students would be assigned to faculty advisers in their own programs of study.

The advising office would work closely with the offices that handle admissions, financial aid, registration, counseling, placement testing, and academic support services, as well as with academic departments. It would have the responsibility for the development, maintenance, and distribution of advising files, for evaluation of the advising system and advisers, for preservice and in-service training for all advisers, for development of both adviser and advisee handbooks, and for coordination of a freshman seminar program.

There are many advantages of this ideal model: (1) It utilizes the best advising resources during the times that are most critical to student success and retention. (2) It provides well-trained advisers with student development backgrounds to assist students during the first semester or year when they are most apt to explore various programs and declare or change majors. (3) It provides the expertise of faculty when students are more settled in their programs and need faculty assistance in making connections among current study, future study, and work. (4) It provides a way of easing heavy faculty advising loads. And (5) it guarantees that advising services are coordinated.

## References

Crockett, D. S. "Academic Advising." In L. Noel, R. Levitz, D. Saluri, and Associates, *Increasing Student Retention: Effective Programs and Practices for Reducing the Dropout Rate*. San Francisco: Jossey-Bass, 1985.

Habley, W. R. "The Advantages and Disadvantages of Using Students as Academic Advisors." *NASPA Journal*, 1979, *17* (1), 46–51.

Habley, W. R. "Organizational Structures for Academic Advising: Models and Implications." *Journal of College Student Personnel*, 1983, *24* (6), 535–540.

Habley, W. R. *The Status and Future of Academic Advising: Problems and Promise*. Iowa City, Iowa: American College Testing, 1988.

Habley, W. R. *Fulfilling the Promise?* Iowa City, Iowa: American College Testing, 1993.

Habley, W. R., and McCauley, M. E. "The Relationship Between Institutional Characteristics and the Organization of Advising Services." *NACADA Journal*, 1987, *7* (1), 27–39.

Kerr, B. "Alumni as Peer Advisers in a Community College." *Journal of College Student Personnel*, 1983, *24*, 366–367.

King, M. C. "Utilizing Part-Time Paraprofessionals as Academic Advisors: A Model." In D. S. Crockett (ed.), *Academic Advising: A Resource Document, 1978 Supplement*. Iowa City, Iowa: American College Testing, 1979. 1,191 pp. (ED 189 906)

Teague, G. V., and Grites, T. J. "Faculty Contracts and Academic Advising. *Journal of College Student Personnel*, 1980, *21* (1), 40–44.

Terenzini, P. T., and Pascarella, E. T. "Student/Faculty Relationships and Freshman Year Educational Outcomes: A Further Investigation." *Journal of College Student Personnel*, 1980, *21* (6), 521–528.

MARGARET C. KING *is assistant dean for student development at Schenectady County Community College, Schenectady, New York. She currently serves as president of the National Academic Advising Association (1991–1993).*

*Adviser training in community colleges serves not only as a powerful retention strategy but also as a team-building staff development activity.*

# Adviser Training in the Community College

*Portia K. Weston*

An academic adviser training program benefits an institution in many ways. Not only does it contribute to more effective advising services for students, which enhance student growth, satisfaction, and persistence, but it also contributes to enhanced communication among faculty and staff.

## The Case for Adviser Training

In developing an adviser training program, it is important, first, to consider the background and position of those receiving the training (Gordon, 1984). For example, a program for counselors would differ significantly from one for faculty. However, no matter whom the program is designed for, an effective training program helps to integrate all advisers into the culture of the college, as members of the educational "team." Adviser training also serves a number of other functions: (1) It builds an understanding of how the various components of the campus interact. (2) It reduces barriers between administrative, academic, and student service functions. (3) It creates an understanding of the contribution of the individual adviser, faculty member, or counselor to the whole process of educating students. For example, the English instructor trained in developmental advising is enabled to see his or her course in the context of a continuum of student learning. The instructor thereby envisions himself or herself as a part of an integrated network of colleagues devoted to the education of students. And (4) it is an effective tool in the process of creating a student-centered institution.

## Effective Adviser Training in Community Colleges

The following components reflect an effective adviser training program:

Clearly stated campuswide mission or policy related to academic advising
Clearly defined objectives and goals of the training program
Sequential sessions, which allow assimilation and affirmation of key concepts
Informational and conceptual content and relational skills
Preservice and in-service training
Evaluation of the training program, with appropriate adjustment based on evaluation

### Informational Content

Informational content is that which the adviser needs to know about the college, including the resources available to enable the student to make appropriate decisions. This content includes

Institutional mission or statement of purpose
Advising mission or statement of purpose
Goals and objectives of the training program
Delivery system of advising services
Printed items: forms, handbooks, fact sheets, and program sheets
College systems: flow of student-institution interaction (referrals, transcript evaluation, and others)
Rules and requirements: policies, degree requirements, prerequisites, exemptions, advanced placement, and others
Resources: financial aid, career planning, counseling, academic support services, disabled student services, college survival courses, health services, minority affairs, job placement, transfer student activities, community liaison services (mental health department, health department), and others
Student information systems: computer or paper-based (how to use; issues regarding confidentiality)
Characteristics of the community college student, both national and local, including age, educational background, and family status
Special populations: returning adults, minorities, and first generation
Particular needs, expectations of special populations
Records and files

### Conceptual Content

Conceptual content refers to what an adviser must understand about the advising process, including the definition of academic advising, adviser and student rights and responsibilities, and the relationship of advising to the institutional mission. Elements included in conceptual content are

Institutional mission or statement of purpose and how the advising system
    enhances or supports it
Advising mission or statement of purpose and how individual advising
    enhances or supports it
Developmental orientation of O'Banion's (1972) advising model
Advisers' rights and responsibilities
Students' rights and responsibilities
Legal implications of advising
Relationship of advising to other services
Student and adviser expectations in the advising process

   In the process of guiding a student through the education system, there are opportunities to enhance the student's development in various life skills. The adviser needs to learn how to guide students in goal setting, decision making, and values clarification.

## Relational Skills for Advisers

Generally, relational skills for advisers refer to behaviors of the adviser in relating to the student. The content includes such topics as (1) interviewing skills: organization of the interview, phases of the interview, interviewing structure as a mechanism for effective use of time; (2) questioning skills, including types of questions (open-closed, leading-neutral, primary-secondary); (3) listening skills: enhancers and barriers, and active listening; (4) nonverbal communication; and (5) referral skills.

## Types of Adviser Training Programs

The most effective training for community college advisers is designed to include sequential sessions. Each session has a distinct focus and builds on previous knowledge gained through the training. If we assume that advisers "develop" in much the same way as students, sequential training is mean-ingful. An effective way to develop master advisers is to require "nuts-and-bolts" informational training before any advising occurs and then to assign the novice adviser advisees of his or her own to work with while progressing through the remaining sessions. It is important in such a process that the novice adviser have support, in the form of either an advising office, a department head, a mentor, or a master adviser. In this way, the new adviser can apply what is learned in the classroom to the real-world context of advising.

   Another method of sequenced training is for new advisers to work through training modules created by the advising office or whoever is responsible for coordinating advising services. These modules may be self-paced units, studied individually or in groups. An advantage of this system is that it provides consistent training to participants; a disadvantage is that it takes quite a bit of time to create modules and keep them current. Other methods for adviser training include the following:

*One-day workshops.* These workshops cover the same topics as sequential training sessions but do so all in one day. Some workshops have follow-up components.

*Mentoring/master adviser.* In this method, a new adviser is assigned to a practicing adviser for a designated period of time. It is assumed that through observation and individual instruction the new adviser will learn the necessary skills and information. A weakness of this system is that it may be inconsistent in its delivery of information and values and may not provide the broader linkages with other components of the campus community. Another version of this method is for a new adviser to participate in a formal training session and then be assigned to a mentor.

*On-the-job training.* Many institutions that say they do not have adviser training programs in fact have on-the-job training programs. Especially in community colleges, where more faculty are required to advise than are required to have training, it is evident that advisers are expected to learn as they go. Obvious weaknesses of this method include perceptions of advising activities as mere matters of scheduling, inconsistency of delivery, inaccurate information, dissatisfaction among those who are asked to perform duties that they feel ill-equipped to manage, and dissatisfaction among students.

Any comprehensive training program should also incorporate ongoing, mandatory, in-service training, including refresher courses on relational and conceptual components of advising and updates on informational components.

## Training Techniques

There are a number of techniques available for training advisers. Exemplary programs employ a variety of techniques, including some that require active participation by advisers. Examples include external presenters (often used to kick off the training program), internal presenters (such as counselors, department chairs, and financial aid staff), discussion groups and brown-bag lunches, panel sessions, brainstorming activities, simulations (videotapes and discussions), and case studies.

## Model Training Outline

The following model training outline was developed at Greenville Technical College and is used to train new university transfer-division faculty and full-time advisers. Each session is approximately two hours in length, and the entire program is spread throughout the academic year. Advisers complete sessions 1 and 2 and are then assigned advisees; consequently, they have already begun working with students when they go through the remaining training sessions.

Session 1: "Nuts and Bolts" (may require two, two-hour sessions)
1. Institutional mission and the mission of the advising system
2. Description of the advising system and rationale for its organization
3. Definition of developmental academic advising
   Review of developmental advising theory
   Why advising is important
4. Responsibilities of the adviser
   Legal responsibilities
   Confidentiality of student records
   Availability to students
   Working with the undecided student
5. Community college student: characteristics
6. Tools for advising
   Adviser's resource book or handbook
   Flowchart showing college systems such as admissions and student
      records
   Prerequisite sheet
   Course list
   College catalogue (required reading)
   Placement testing, including procedures, test interpretation, and use
      of results
7. Role of advising center
8. Question and answer
9. Advising center tour

Session 2: Student Records
1. Questions (from prior session)
2. How to access the student records system (paper or computer)
3. Information available to advisers
4. Responsibilities of the adviser in regard to record maintenance and
   confidentiality

Session 3: Resources
1. Questions (from prior sessions)
2. Referrals
   Definition of referral (it is not only for problems!)
   When to refer
   How to make an effective referral
   Legal responsibilities (review)

3. Types of referrals and identification of individuals and offices appropriate for each

    Academic issues

    Financial concerns

    Health concerns

    Logistics problems

        Transportation

        Housing

        Child care

    Choosing a career, major, or transfer

    Personal concerns

        Counselors on campus

        Outside agencies

        Disabled services

        Student activities

Session 4: Relational Issues

1. Questions (from prior sessions)
2. Overview of the communication process

    Verbal

    Nonverbal

3. Interviews

    Basic organization

    Types of questions

4. Listening

    Barriers to effective listening

    Results of poor listening

    Active listening

5. Personality types: understanding one's own style and how that affects advising relationships

    Abbreviated Myers-Briggs personality inventory

    Personality type and relationships

6. Relational skills to develop with advisees

    Helping students identify goals

    Helping students clarify values

    Helping students make decisions

Session 5: Advising as a Means of Enhancing Student Growth and Retention

1. Review of previous sessions: reemphasize mission statements (institutional and advising)
2. Question and answer (from prior sessions)
3. Advising as means of retention: role-play situations where the adviser could intervene

4. Final exam! Advising as a developmental process (ungraded quiz where adviser identifies developmental advising behaviors)

## Conclusion

It is clear that community colleges need to address the issue of adviser training. Effective adviser training is an imperative in any strong, effective advising program. As an increasing number of institutions begin to develop comprehensive advising programs, they must also develop training programs with components that serve the needs of the student, the adviser, and the institution. Adviser training must also take into account the characteristics, skills, and abilities of those receiving the training. The training program should focus on the development of effective advising skills. Those institutions that address adviser training carefully are those that reap the broad benefits of enhanced student satisfaction and persistence and enhanced communication among all segments of the college community.

## References

Gordon, V. N. "Training Professional and Paraprofessional Advisors." In R. B. Winston, Jr., and others, *Developmental Academic Advising: Addressing Students' Educational, Career, and Personal Needs*. San Francisco: Jossey-Bass, 1984.

O'Banion, T. "An Academic Advising Model." *Junior College Journal*, 1972, 42 (6), 62, 64, 66–69.

PORTIA K. WESTON *is former department head of orientation, advising, and counseling at Greenville Technical College, Greenville, South Carolina. She is currently an English instructor and academic adviser at Clemson University.*

*Evaluation of the advising system and of the advisers and recognition
and reward for effective advising are key components of an institutional
advising program.*

# Evaluation, Recognition, and Reward of Academic Advising

*Buddy Ramos*

The purpose of this chapter is to examine the role of evaluation and of
recognition and reward in the organization and delivery of academic advising in the community college. I discuss the many benefits for students,
advisers, and administrators that can come from implementing an evaluation process and identify factors that must be considered in doing so.

If an institution is going to undertake an evaluation program, it cannot
be done in isolation. If an institution does not have an adviser training
(development) program in place, then it does not make sense to evaluate
individuals who have not been informed about how to perform their
responsibilities or programs. Moreover, an institution must convey the
importance of academic advising to advisers by recognizing and rewarding
their efforts in the field of advising. The needs of students and prospective
students place a heavy demand on advising services in the community
college. Advisers generally are student-oriented and work hard in helping
students achieve their goals. While advisers experience many intrinsic
rewards from working with students, the likelihood of adviser burnout is
increased if some manner of external recognition and reward is not present.

## Assessment and Evaluation

The existence of a developmental advising program does not necessarily
mean the presence of an evaluation process. Recently, I visited the campus
of a well-respected midwestern community college for the purpose of giving
the advising staff feedback concerning their academic advising system. The
system was impressive in many respects: Advisers practiced developmental

academic advising, the mission was clearly stated, and there were substantial publications, facilities, and computer support. When asked questions about how students felt about the advisers and the advising system, the level of satisfaction with advising, and which measures were used to ascertain the effectiveness of the advising on campus, the nature of the response was, "Well, we tried an evaluation a few years ago and no one really liked it; and anyway we know we are doing a good job." While this type of response is certainly disappointing, it is not surprising. In fact, it was well illustrated by the four national surveys on academic advising conducted by the American College Testing (ACT) Program in 1979, 1983, 1987, and, most recently, 1991. The good news is that since the first survey, there has been a steady increase in the number of community colleges reporting institutional engagement in a regularly scheduled method of evaluating advising on their campuses. The bad news is that approximately six out of ten institutions do not undertake systematic evaluation of the effectiveness of their advising programs. In addition, evaluation of individual advisers is also not particularly common (Habley, 1988, p. 54).

If we expect a quality product, we need to check periodically on the status of that product. Why does this notion seem to fall apart when applied to academic advising? Certainly, there is ample documentation of the positive impact of academic advising on a student's academic performance and personal satisfaction with his or her college experience (Winston and others, 1984). Evaluation of academic advising can enhance advising services and can be used to develop a needs assessment, reorganize personnel, and plan future administrative policy (Grites and Kramer, 1984). Additionally, evaluation results can support merit recognition raises, promote budget changes or increased administrative support, point out areas of need for inservice training, and determine effectiveness of advisers and advising programs (Crockett, 1983). Many evaluations have addressed the positive relationship that exists between good advising and student retention (Noel, 1985; Forrest, 1985).

## Considerations in the Design and Implementation of an Evaluation Program

The National Academic Advising Association (NACADA, 1989) in a position paper on assessment provides all institutional types with key questions to consider and specific guidelines and recommendations in implementing an evaluation process on college campuses. The predominant themes outlined in the NACADA position paper are as follows: First, the context for evaluating advising should include standards and guidelines for evaluation of both individual advisers and advising programs. In the evaluation of individual advisers, NACADA proposes eight components of developmental advising that need to be assessed: (1) assist students in self-understanding and self-acceptance (values clarification, understanding of abilities, interests, and limitations); (2) assist students in their consideration of life goals by relating interests, skills, abilities, and values to careers, the world of work, and the nature and purpose of higher education; (3) assist students in developing education plans consistent with life goals and objectives (alternative courses of action, alternate career considerations, and selection of courses); (4) assist students in developing decision-making skills; (5) provide accurate information about institutional policies, procedures, resources, and programs; (6) make referrals to other institutional or community support services; (7) assist students in initial and continuing evaluation of progress toward established goals and education plans; and (8) provide information about students either individually or collectively to the institution, colleges, or academic departments. In terms of these eight factors, it is apparent that NACADA recommends that advisers receive feedback on the extent to which their advising is developmental. In fact, the first three components listed are the first steps identified in O'Banion's (1972) model of academic advising, a model often credited with establishing the concept of developmental academic advising.

Second, NACADA suggests that advising programs measure their effectiveness based on the following criteria:

*Mission:* Is the purpose of advising clearly stated, known, and regularly reviewed? Is the mission of advising related directly to the mission of the institution? Are the mission of the institution and purpose of advising stated in the catalogue for students to read?

*Selection:* What are the criteria for selecting advisers? Is the process open, clear, and regularly reviewed?

*Orientation and training:* Is there initial and ongoing training of those who serve as advisers? Is this training updated and reviewed regularly?

*Communication:* What is the process for sending and receiving information about the advising system and advisees? Is the information adequate, complete, clear, and available in a regular and timely fashion?

*Reward and recognition of the individual adviser:* Is there an established, known, and operating system of evaluating advisers, recognizing strengths and weaknesses and rewarding accordingly?

*Evaluation of the advising system:* Is there an established, understood, and effective system of evaluating the advising program, recognizing strengths and weaknesses and distributing resources accordingly? Are the data gathered regularly acted on?

*Needs assessment:* Is there a regular process to assess the needs of the system, the advisers, the students, and the institution? Is there a way of regularly, adequately, and correctly obtaining necessary data about advising?

*Delivery system:* Is there a structured, clear, predictable, and efficient academic advising delivery system? Is it known to others at the institution, especially potential advisees? Is the process regularly reviewed to ensure that it is effective and achieving the mission and goals?

*Support:* What is the level of support for the advising program in such areas as budget, staffing, publicity, and consultation? Is the advising program supported by faculty, administrators, other advisers, advisees, and related campus personnel?

*Resources:* Are there sufficient resources such as facilities, books, staff, and computers to enable the mission of the advising system to be fulfilled? Is the question of resource adequacy regularly reviewed?

*Critical issues:* Are such matters as confidentiality, access to advising, and fairness in advising considered and dealt with as part of the advising system? Is there an accepted code of conduct and a system whereby such issues can be raised and addressed?

An effective evaluation program not only provides the student with an opportunity to assess the advising services that he or she has received but also provides an opportunity for advisers, administrators, and faculty to have input into the process. Perspectives of all members of the campus community have value and should be used in making important decisions. Probably the most critical factor an institution must consider in implementing an evaluation program is how results of the evaluations are to be used. It is my belief that the primary use of an evaluation process is to improve advising individually and programmatically, thereby enhancing advising services and student satisfaction.

Institutions need broad support on their campuses in order to implement an evaluation process. Several factors should be considered when building this support. First and most essential is administrative support. Without such support, the likelihood of a meaningful evaluation program is remote. Second, the advisers should have input into the evaluation program. When advisers are included in the selection or development of an evaluation instrument and in the design of the process, they have greater ownership of the program. Another area for adviser input is the determination of how the evaluation results are to be used. Results may be used in either a formative or summative manner. Formative evaluation involves provision of feedback at regular intervals to improve the advising process. Summative evaluation is designed to help administrators arrive at final judgments concerning the advising process. Whichever method is chosen, consensus will be more easily obtained if those who are to be involved are participants in the development of the evaluation program.

## Evaluation Model at Johnson County Community College

The purpose of focusing here on the evaluation process at Johnson County Community College (JCCC), in Overland Park, Kansas, is not to suggest that it is the ideal model. Rather, it illustrates one institution's attempt to implement some of the principles previously mentioned. As institutions become involved in an evaluation program, they will readily discover that it is an evolving process. Mistakes will be made and modifications will be necessary. Flexibility is an important ingredient.

Academic advising at JCCC is delivered by professional counselors located in a centralized location. For the sake of clarity, advisers are referred to here as "counselors." Students are seen on a walk-in basis, but they may also make appointments with their counselors. Evaluation of advising at JCCC consists of four primary methods: five-year program review, annual telephone survey, student evaluation form, and supervisor performance review.

**Five-Year Program Review.** The five-year program review provides the JCCC Counseling Center with the opportunity to evaluate its perceived effectiveness in the following areas: mission, service area functions, service area clientele, accreditation, service evaluation, facilities and equipment, personnel, financial resources, methods and technology, community service and participation, professional activities, and professional development.

The center rates itself in each area on a scale from "very strong" and "satisfactory" to "needs improvement," "major concern," and "not applicable." Supporting documentation and written comments may also be used to further explain any one of the ratings. This summative form of evaluation gives the center a valuable opportunity to highlight for the administration some of the significant contributions of the center during the previous five-year period. More important, this information is used to identify deficiencies and to establish the need for more space, additional staff, increased technological support, more staff development opportunities, and so on.

**Telephone Survey.** The annual telephone survey of students is the second method by which the counseling center evaluates its advising services. This survey is conducted (typically in November) by a private market-interviewing firm hired by the college in conjunction with the JCCC Institutional Research Office. Survey recipients are randomly selected and are asked the following questions:

"How often have you used the counseling center within the last year?"
"Why didn't you use the counseling center? Was it because . . . ?"
"In what way was it inconvenient? Was it . . . ?"
"How would you rate (excellent, good, average, fair, or poor) the counseling center on each of the following?:
> *Attitude of staff:* Was the staff helpful, friendly, courteous, pleasant, and so on?
> *Knowledge or competence of the staff:* Did they know what they were doing? Did you get your questions answered?
> *Accessibility:* How easy was it to use the service (hours, days, location, and so on)?

*Your overall satisfaction:* Did you get what you wanted? What would you say are the primary strengths of this service? What would you say are the primary weaknesses of this service?"

Replies to the questions are then tabulated and the verbal responses are transcribed. Results are given to the dean of students and the program director of counseling, who then shares them with the entire counseling staff.

This formative evaluation allows the entire counseling center staff (receptionist, secretaries, student development assistants, and counselors) to receive feedback about how well the system is working from the standpoint of the most important source, the student.

**Student Evaluation Form.** Counselors are evaluated by students on a monthly basis. By random selection, ten students per counselor receive an evaluation form in the mail. These students are selected from counseling center sign-in sheets on which all students are asked to record their names and social security numbers. Upon completion of the evaluation form, it is mailed back to the JCCC Institutional Research Office, where the results are tabulated and verbatim comments transcribed. Once a year, each counselor receives his or her student evaluation results and is able to compare his or her individual performance to mean scores for all the counselors in the center.

The evaluation form allows students to rate counselors on a scale from "excellent" and "above average" to "average," "below average," "poor," and "not applicable" on the following categories: (1) *Professional manner:* Did counselor show courtesy, genuine interest, and respect and listen carefully? (2) *Knowledge:* Was counselor knowledgeable about JCCC courses and programs, transferring to colleges and universities, educational and career opportunities, JCCC policies and procedures, and resources and services at JCCC? (3) *Effectiveness:* Did counselor help resolve a problem or question satisfactorily, achieve a realistic understanding of options available, and so on? There is also an overall rating.

The counseling center is also able to gather information from the student regarding the nature of the contact (that is, career, personal, and so on) and demographic information such as sex, age, and part-time versus full-time and day versus evening enrollment. Students are also asked to answer either "yes," "no," or "not sure" to the following questions: "In general, did you get the help that you needed?" "Would you consult with this counselor again, or would you recommend this person to someone else needing similar help?"

Students also have the opportunity to make any additional comments concerning the counselor with whom they have met. The results of this evaluation are used strictly in a formative manner. Counselors benefit from comparing their own performance from year to year and appear to take great pride in observing improvements in specific areas.

This evaluation process, more so than any other at JCCC, has required the most effort to design, implement, and maintain. Additionally, the program has evolved into its present form with many modifications, primarily in details of process. The most important ingredient in the success of this program has been the involvement of the counselors. Counselors were included in the design of the evaluation form and in the process of how the forms are administered and delivered. Without their input, this program would never have become a reality.

**Supervisor Performance Review.** The review by the program director of counseling provides feedback to the counselors regarding their performance. It is a summative evaluation in which all aspects of the individual counselor's work, such as student contact, committee work, and courses taught, are considered. The evaluation is also used in the rehiring process.

## Summary of Evaluation

As previously stated, the most important aspect of an evaluation program is planning how the results will be used to improve the advising program and thereby positively affect students' lives. Evaluation is best seen not as a threat but rather as a powerful tool that involves gathering information on appropriate structures, processes, personnel, and activities in order to determine through careful study and appraisal their significance and value (National Academic Advising Association, 1989).

## Recognition and Reward of Academic Advising

It is not surprising that the recognition and reward of academic advising in the community college (and in all institutional types) has consistently ranked lowest on all four of the ACT Program's national surveys in terms of how advising programs rated their own effectiveness. In the third survey (Habley, 1988), respondents were asked to consider both the current effectiveness and the progress made in the prior five years on the following eleven organizational and administrative variables: advisee information, meeting of students' needs, adviser traits, campuswide communication, program economy, adviser selection, campuswide coordination, accountability, training, evaluation, and recognition and reward.

Not only is recognition and reward still considered the least effective area of endeavor, it is also the area in which the least amount of progress has occurred. While the reasons for this may vary depending on the structure and culture of individual campuses, some of the overriding factors are as follows:

*Lack of administrative support.* Without administrative support, all other efforts to reward advisers are destined to fail. Administrators must be convinced of the positive effects that good advising can have on students and the institution as a whole. Strategies to enlist this support will differ from institution to institution. Recommendations for developing this support are given later in this chapter.

*Lack of an effective adviser training and evaluation program.* As previously stated, without adequate training and evaluation, it is senseless, if not impossible, to reward effective advisers. This recognition and reward process develops from the ground up. If people are not prepared to properly perform their jobs and are unclear about job expectations, how can they be fairly evaluated? If individuals are not evaluated, on what basis are they to be rewarded?

*Lack of recognition of advising as an integral part of a faculty member's responsibility.* This factor is more of a concern for models in which advising is performed by a decentralized faculty as opposed to a centralized professional advising staff whose primary mission is to advise students. In a faculty-based system, advising is often expected of faculty yet is given little or no consideration as part of tenure or promotion decisions. If it is, it is weighed very lightly. Nor is effective advising recognized in other ways. Advisers and administrators must correct this situation.

*Lack of knowledge of an appropriate reward structure.* If administrators determine what is appropriate for a reward and the advisers do not value this choice, nothing has really been accomplished. Therefore, a necessary and important first step in developing a recognition and reward scheme is to involve the advisers in order to ensure that the reward is viewed as meaningful. Following is a list of possible approaches to faculty adviser recognition and reward methods, together with the percentages of community colleges utilizing them as reported from the 1987 ACT survey (Habley, 1988, p. 42):

Release time from instruction (4.3 percent)
Release time from committee work (1.1 percent)
Release time from research expectations (1.1 percent)
Salary increments for time spent in advising (2.1 percent)
Major consideration in promotion and tenure (2.1 percent)
Minor consideration in promotion and tenure (6.4 percent)
Awards for excellence in advising (1.1 percent)

Institutions must be innovative in their approaches to the recognition and reward of advising activities. They need not be restricted to the forms of recognition and reward listed above, and institutions can speak most loudly by allocating some budgetary consideration for an effective recognition and reward program.

## Suggestions for Implementing a Recognition and Reward Program

Puffer (1990) has suggested eight ways to develop an effective service reward system. Although not designed specifically for advising or even for an educational setting, the process merits attention. Puffer's (1990, pp. 8–12) eight general guidelines for developing a recognition and reward program are as follows:

*Define objectives.* Is the primary purpose of a recognition and reward program to improve productivity? Lower error rates? Improve customer service? Basically, what is to be accomplished by implementing such a program? A clear definition of these objectives in ways that show how the organization and staff will benefit helps people at various levels buy into the program and helps to enlist vital support from top management.

*Lead by management example.* Top management needs to make a total and continuing commitment to recognition and reward programs. Without this commitment, staff see the efforts, however well intentioned, as empty gestures.

*Develop specific criteria.* Good criteria define the specific kind of performance that will be rewarded and provide measurable guidelines to help track and fine-tune the program over time. Goals must be challenging, yet achievable for all concerned.

*Use meaningful rewards.* Puffer stresses the point that no reward and recognition program can adequately compensate for low salary levels. Further, the institution must recognize that today's worker is often motivated by such things as equity, status, power, family and leisure time, and self-development. A combination of awards, workplace perks, public recognition, and written commendations can be very effective.

*Involve staff.* Involvement of staff in the early stages of planning and throughout the entire process helps to ensure that they will be more dedicated to the success of the program.

*Keep communications clear.* If recognition and reward programs are going to be effective, they need to be understood. Use kickoff events, periodic updates, and internal communication channels to keep people informed and enthused. It is important to ask for feedback and to listen to staff as the program grows and changes.

*Reward teams.* Rewarding of teams rather than of individual efforts may allow everyone on a team to share equally in a reward when a goal is met. Or a combination of team effort and individual reward can be established.

*Manage over the long term.* To succeed over time, recognition programs should be part of a comprehensive effort to improve institutional performance. The desire to improve service quality, productivity, and so on must become part of the overall institutional philosophy. Otherwise, recognition programs become flash-in-the-pan affairs that occur whenever there is a problem but have no lasting benefit to the institution.

Puffer's guidelines help institutions to consider important factors before embarking on a recognition program. Certainly, institutions will have to develop their own strategies based on an understanding of their particular institutional cultures and the available resources.

Jerry Steiner from Chemeketa Community College in Salem, Oregon, with the assistance of Maricopa County Community College, Tempe, Arizona; Kirkwood Community College, Cedar Rapids, Iowa; Johnson County Community College, Overland Park, Kansas; Santa Fe Community College, Gainesville, Florida; Central Piedmont Community College, Charlotte, North Carolina; and Dallas County Community College, Dallas, Texas, has compiled a list of ideas for recognizing community college staff contributions (Steiner, 1990). A partial list of these ideas follows:

Cash merit awards ($100–$1,000) or in-kind personal computer hardware or software for specific projects or an accumulation of special projects awarded by the dean.

Presidential awards, including engraved pen or pen-and-pencil sets, restaurant dinner certificates for groups or individuals, and coastal motel certificates awarded for special achievement or merit as appropriate.

Quarterly bulletin board display called "Street of Stars," recognizing staff members for various special achievements or outstanding performance.

Annual ceremony to recognize staff, including presentation of special pins for one, five, ten, fifteen, or twenty years of service, and special plaques for retirees (note that colleges may vary on years of service).

Special annual awards with special plaques: a presidential award to recognize a staff member who has shown exemplary service to the college staff, students, or the public; an Innovator of the Year award to recognize a staff member who has designed an innovative approach, program, or process.

Staff nominate fellow staff members to a committee for selecting an "ambassador" award recipient to recognize special accomplishments, ideas, extra efforts, good deeds, and other outstanding activities that take place throughout the year.

Each campus annually selects one outstanding staff member in each of the following areas: faculty, administration, support personnel, part-time faculty, and maintenance and crafts.

Each campus annually selects one collegewide Innovator of the Year. A districtwide innovator is also selected among the various campuses.

Survey is conducted of all graduates as well as nongraduates who have completed fifty hours or more but are no longer students. From the information received, a brochure is published with pictures of ten to fifteen faculty and quotes from students citing the differences that those faculty members have made in their lives.

Quarterly publication highlighting eight to twelve staff members and their positions within the college, including staff from all areas of the college community.

Staff members may nominate staff for "extra effort" awards to recognize those who go "above and beyond" for the good of the college, with a presentation ceremony in the president's office.

## Conclusion

The evaluation and assessment of individual advisers and advising programs is essential for the development of stronger advising services in the community college. A program to recognize and reward individual advisers and advising systems for exemplary service will do much to enhance the status of these individuals and systems and as a result improve the quality of service provided to students.

Progress in these areas has been slow over the last decade, but it is showing signs of improvement. Community colleges, because of a unique ability to respond quickly to needs in higher education, can provide the leadership for all colleges and universities to develop and implement evaluation and recognition programs. The more that these topics are discussed, written about, and presented at conferences, the greater the likelihood that all institutions will see the benefit of engaging in such activities and thereby advance the status of academic advising in higher education.

## References

Crockett, D. S. "Assessing Your Advising Program." In D. S. Crockett (ed.), *Advising Skills Techniques and Resources.* (Rev. ed.) Iowa City, Iowa: American College Testing and ACT National Center for Advancement of Educational Practices, 1983.

Forrest, A. "Creating Conditions for Student and Institutional Success." In L. Noel, R. Levitz, D. Saluri, and Associates, *Increasing Student Retention: Effective Programs and Practices for Reducing the Dropout Rate.* San Francisco: Jossey-Bass, 1985.

Grites, T. J., and Kramer, G. "Conducting a Self-Study of Your Advising Program." Unpublished manuscript, Stockton State College, Pomona, N.J., 1984.

Habley, W. R. (ed.). *The Status and Future of Academic Advising: Problems and Promise.* Iowa City, Iowa: American College Testing, 1988.

National Academic Advising Association. *Task Force on Assessment.* Newark: National Academic Advising Association, University of Delaware, 1989.

Noel, L. "Increasing Student Retention: New Challenges and Potential." In L. Noel, R. Levitz, D. Saluri, and Associates, *Increasing Student Retention: Effective Programs and Practices for Reducing the Dropout Rate.* San Francisco: Jossey-Bass, 1985.

O'Banion, T. "An Academic Advising Model." *Junior College Journal,* 1972, 42 (6), 62, 64, 66–69.

Puffer, T. "Eight Ways to Construct Effective Service Reward Systems." *Reward and Recognition,* Aug. 1990, pp. 8–12.

Steiner, J. "Ideas to Recognize Community College Staff for Their Contributions." Unpublished manuscript, Chemeketa Community College, Salem, Oregon, 1990.

Winston, R. B., Jr., and others. *Developmental Academic Advising: Addressing Students' Educational, Career, and Personal Needs.* San Francisco: Jossey-Bass, 1984.

*BUDDY RAMOS is director of the counseling center at Johnson County Community College, Overland Park, Kansas. He is currently completing his doctorate in higher education at the University of Kansas, Lawrence.*

*There are specific factors to consider and strategies to employ when advising students in two-year colleges.*

# Advising the Two-Year Student: Considerations and Strategies

*Judith L. Sanford-Harris*

The adviser at a community college or junior college has a difficult job—that of guiding students through a relatively brief but intense encounter with that institution. The adviser must establish a relationship with the advisee, assist the advisee in understanding the systems and the expectations of that college, and help the advisee accomplish his or her goals in what is traditionally thought of as a two-year program. For individuals who are new to advising, the task can seem overwhelming. The strategies offered herein were developed with the new adviser in mind but may be used by any adviser with any student population.

How do we advise students in a two-year, open-enrollment institution? How do we meet the many and varied needs of the students? How do we help them to determine where they are going (for example, transfer, career after two years, or dual degree) in just two years? What issues must we consider in working with such students? What are some of the strategies that can assist us in the advising process?

Graduation with an associate degree after two years of study is less and less the norm. More colleges and universities are enrolling increasing numbers of nontraditional students: older students, women in technical fields, first-generation college students, multicultural students, and students of color. Family, work, and financial obligations have made a full-time course load less realistic for large numbers of these students. For example, at Bunker Hill Community College, an urban, public community college in Boston, where I serve as dean, only 30 percent of the students take five courses per semester and only 17 percent complete the associate degree in two years; 50 percent take three to five years to complete the associate or "two-year" degree. It is therefore important to discuss with the student that while an associate degree can be completed in two years, it is not necessary to do so. Such a discussion at the start of an advising relationship will go a long way in relieving the pressure and the guilt that many new students feel when they realize that they will not be able to carry a full course load and complete a degree in two years.

Students come to two-year colleges for a variety of reasons. For some, the need or desire to stay close to home and to save on the cost of tuition may be paramount. Many come planning to transfer to a four-year institution to earn a baccalaureate degree and are preoccupied with concerns about transferability of courses. Others enroll in career-oriented programs, hoping to move quickly into the job market. Their concerns appropriately relate to the job opportunities available after degree completion. And still others come with little or no idea of what their goals are or how best to attain them.

The above situations are even more complicated when students need remedial courses to enhance their basic skills. It may be difficult for some students to understand or accept the fact that developmental courses may be required before they can register for courses that count toward the degree. Students may resent the institution for pointing out such shortcomings or may be embarrassed at their lack of college-level skills. Many will be concerned that enrollment in developmental courses will only delay them further in achieving their transfer or career goals and will resist adviser recommendations, insisting that "things are different now" and "I can do it." All of these situations present challenges to the adviser.

## Questions

In advising any student, it is helpful to keep the following questions in mind throughout the advising process. Is transfer an option or consideration? Students need to be alerted to issues related to transfer and also encouraged to view transfer as an option early in the advising process.

Are there additional academic requirements for the advisee who hopes to transfer to a particular college? Articulation agreements with some colleges and universities may require specific courses above and beyond those required for graduation. In order to satisfy those requirements, a student in a tightly defined program might have to take as many as twelve to fifteen additional credits. Where such transfer requirements exist, advance planning is a must. It is helpful to place the graduation and transfer requirements side by side, or to superimpose one over the other, in order to determine where to fit in any additional requirements. Students with such plans should be encouraged to maintain contact with the receiving colleges and with the home institution's transfer office until graduation. Colleges with computerized degree audits have a decided advantage when this type of planning is needed. The degree audit can accommodate any "what if" scenario, including the possibility of a failed course, or changes of major with a resulting change in required courses.

Must the advisee complete the associate degree if he or she wants to transfer? While many articulation agreements require an associate degree if a student hopes to enter the receiving institution with junior status, the student can transfer to many institutions without first earning the degree. It is important to remember, however, that for some students the associate degree and the accompanying graduation are necessary symbols of accomplishment, sources of immediate gratification. It may be helpful in that situation to discuss the benefits of completing the degree and weighing them against the benefits of transferring after two or three semesters or quarters.

How certain is the student of his or her education and career plans and how has he or she arrived at those decisions? If the student is undecided, reassurance should be given that indecision is normal, and suggestions should be made regarding resources available to assist in that decision making. The adviser and the student should also look at available programs with career and transfer tracks and options. A freshman unsure of his or her plans should be encouraged to keep future options open. If possible, the advisee should be encouraged to try to take courses for both programs, at least until a decision is made as to which track is preferred. Again, the task is to superimpose one program over the other to identify the differences, and then determine whether it is practical to expect completion of those courses.

How many semesters does the advisee wish to spend in order to achieve whatever goals are defined? Some students believe that they are failures if they do not complete a degree in two years. Some jobs may require that a student complete a degree before a designated date in order to be eligible for certain benefits or pay increases, so special planning may be required to achieve that goal.

What are the students' financial resources and have they applied for financial aid? If a student is not eligible for financial aid, how much money does he or she have available? If a student has to pay additional tuition for a fifth, sixth, or even seventh course taken in a given semester, that factor also must be considered. Also, if summer or continuing education courses are less costly, they should be pursued as an option.

Are there parental or other external pressures (spouse, job, and friends) pushing the advisee toward a particular program or degree? Hints of such pressure might be identified in early discussions of education and career plans, but they may also come up when planning the next semester's course strategy. Determine what the advisee's ideas and interests might be and then offer objective information about courses and programs that will help him or her make a decision.

If placement tests are required, how did the student perform? Test results or previous performance in writing, mathematics, or courses with significant reading components may preclude a schedule with two or three reading courses in a semester, or the inclusion of a course such as account-ing, which assumes basic reading and mathematical ability. In many cases, the student will need to be advised to take remedial courses to enhance his or her skills. The adviser must try to help the student understand the importance of basic skills to success in college-level courses and may need to cite institutional statistics that show the success rate of students who successfully complete developmental courses versus those who do not. Students need to realize that it is not uncommon to need such courses and that the courses are there to benefit, not punish, them. Above all, students should be encouraged not to overload themselves and need to be made aware that failing of prerequisite courses can change significantly the strategies or plans that have been worked out.

## Strategies

For students entering an institution unsure of their future and hoping to "find" themselves, the strategies described below may be particularly help-ful. They are, in fact, useful for any student but are crucial for the student who is seeking self.

**Goal Setting.** Goal setting is important in many situations, but espe-cially where the student's education and career goals are vague, are not based on much thought, research, evidence, or experience, or are totally unreal-istic. The student should be able to delineate more clearly his or her long-term goals over time, trying certain courses "on for size," gathering information in a nonthreatening environment, and possibly trying intern-ships. In the beginning, however, it is important to help the student develop several short-term goals that will allow some success in a relatively short period of time. This approach helps to keep the student motivated. Only after the student has met with some success in achieving the short-term goals should a long-term goal be attempted.

Goal setting is not a difficult process. The advisee can be guided through a few basic steps with the use of a worksheet that can be reviewed on a regular basis and adjusted as needed. The worksheet should include the following items: (1) goal description, (2) objectives and an explanation of why each is important, (3) rewards expected, (4) difficulties anticipated or encountered, (5) resources needed, (6) steps to be taken to reach goal (including timetable and completion date), and (7) new directions to take upon reaching the goal. Once the adviser and advisee agree on a goal, the advisee should be asked to consider any difficulties that might be encoun-tered in achieving that goal and to note them on the worksheet. He or she must also agree on dates by which certain tasks are to be completed and on an appropriate deadline for attempting to accomplish the goal. The advisee must then meet with the adviser on a predetermined schedule (daily, biweekly) to discuss current progress toward the goal and to determine whether any modifications in the goal or the timetable are needed. By approaching each goal in a series of small steps, the student is less likely to be overwhelmed at the start or discouraged by small setbacks.

The process of goal setting can be particularly effective with an advisee who has set an unrealistic goal. By working through the various steps on the worksheet, the student may become aware of obstacles (possibly for the first time) or may acknowledge the fact that the goal needs to be modified. For example, the advisee who is attempting to juggle myriad responsibilities while struggling through a nursing program may finally agree that changes in some part of his or her life must be made if the goal of successfully completing the program is eventually to be reached.

Not all goals must be academic. The student may want to learn to be more assertive (which can have an impact on speaking up in class) or to change jobs (which may allow a better schedule or allow an evening course that the student needs) or to lose weight (which would enhance self-esteem). The process of setting goals and the feeling of accomplishment after reaching those goals, in addition to resolving problems for the student, can have a strong positive impact on an advisee's feelings of self-confidence. After reaching one or two goals, a student may have more faith in his or her ability to continue to strive toward a long-term goal that is attainable but requires some persistence.

**Decision-Making Techniques.** Decision-making techniques also can assist the adviser and the student in the advising process. Traditional students in particular often rely on parents, other relatives, or friends to help them to make decisions or to tell them what to do. It is not unusual for adult women to be pressured by spouses or friends about programs that would be "appropriate" for them. And, unfortunately, many minority students continue to be discouraged from pursuing certain programs and careers by guidance counselors, employers, and even faculty and staff.

Very often, advisees expect their advisers to make important decisions for them. One of the most valuable tools that an adviser can offer an advisee is that of learning to make informed, rational decisions on his or her own. Students must be helped to understand that they ultimately must make program choices, consider career and transfer options, and weigh the advice offered by others. Learning how to make decisions and feeling personal satisfaction with a commitment to those decisions can build students' self-confidence and reduce their dependence on the adviser or on significant others when making decisions.

Most of us have developed a style of decision making that we may feel works for us. Those styles can be thought of as parts of a continuum, with those who follow their intuition at one end, and those who use a mathematical or flowchart model or a rigidly structured system of weighing pros and cons at the other end. It is important that the advisee be encouraged to gather concrete information and that discussion center around the real and perceived benefits, and drawbacks, of any decision. It is important that the adviser avoid as much as possible the expression of personal preferences or judgments about any choice. It is helpful, however, for the adviser to suggest points at which the advisee may wish to seek additional information or to try certain steps before a final decision is made. Library research, interviews with potential employers, internships in possible fields of interest, discussions with alumni in certain jobs, and career services resources, for example, are all possible sources of information that can be used again and again as a student attempts to decide on a major. The important point is that the adviser should provide support and encouragement and act as a sounding board as the advisee narrows down his or her options and eventually makes a decision.

A technique that can be nicely tied to decision making is the use of a log/reflections sheet (see Figure 7.1). Such an exercise gives the student an opportunity to consider ideas and likes and dislikes, and to see, in concrete form, a summary of her or his experiences. Figure 7.1 illustrates the reflections of a student who is able to make connections among different courses and to narrow down career possibilities for further investigation.

**Group Advising.** Group advising can be a very helpful tool. Students at commuter colleges often work in a vacuum, coming to the campus each day only long enough to attend class. They often try to muddle through on their own or seek the advice of family and friends, who may not always support their efforts or who may offer erroneous information. Group advising can be helpful because it provides the students with an opportunity to hear from peers in the same or similar situations. Returning women students, minority students, and older students can all benefit from such group sessions. At the same time, the adviser is spared having to repeat the same basic information to every advisee. The students do some of the work for the adviser by sharing ideas and offering suggestions and moral support to one another. The adviser serves as moderator, offers information that might be of interest to the advisees, and makes appropriate referrals for more information and assistance when necessary. Group meetings may be held as frequently as the adviser and the group decide. Meetings may be held during a meal or snack to make the gathering less formal or can be called "brown-bag lunches" in an office or lounge.

If group advising is not appropriate or practical, regularly scheduled departmental meetings for all of the students with the same major may be another alternative. Invite staff from various student services offices, including career planning and placement and the transfer advisers, to meet with the group and talk about career options, the students' marketability, available support services, skills developed in liberal arts and other courses, transferability of courses, and so on. Nontraditional students in particular are often hesitant to seek career and resource information. Such a meeting can provide them with valuable information and help them to formulate questions that they can also discuss with their advisers.

## Figure 7.1. Log/Reflections

Name _____ Semester _____

| Course, Workshop Programs | Skills, Interests Developed Through This Experience | Values, Attitudes, Beliefs Discovered, Confirmed, or Altered | Directions | Areas Worth Exploring/ Possible New Goals |
|---|---|---|---|---|
| ENG 102 B grade | Writing skills improved Critical interpretation | Realized that others my age are concerned about the problem of hazardous waste. | Didn't like writing but did like the films and the analysis of them in class discussions. | A film course might be interesting—maybe journalism? |
| BIO 101 B− | Lab methods Scientific analysis Use of microscope | Can now understand why people go into research as a career. | Not sure I want to go into bio any further, although the labs were interesting. | Maybe a different lab science? |
| Media Career Panel | Learned that there's a lot in this field I wasn't aware of—also, a lot of pressure and long hours. | I've always thought this is an exciting area and would like to know more; the panelists confirmed that it is exciting. | Take some film courses! Maybe an internship? | Maybe I can be a film critic for a newspaper, which would mean I'd have to work on my writing skills. |
| Drug Program | Realized that it's a complex and some-times fascinating problem, especially alcohol abuse. | Realized that I don't want to get involved. | | None |

## Conclusion

The task of helping community and junior college students to plan logically and to make the most of their time at their colleges is complicated by the rapid changes in the student population, such as the demographic shift from traditional to nontraditional students. These changes necessitate the adviser's increasing consideration of important factors such as financial resources and the number of semesters that the student is able to devote to his or her college education, in addition to the usual concerns related to career and transfer planning.

The approach of teaching advisees to consider the future in a self-directed, systematic way can improve greatly not only the student's self-confidence but also the adviser/advisee relationship. It dispels any inappropriate expectations of the advisee concerning the adviser's role, and it develops planning skills that the student will be able to use throughout his or her life.

JUDITH L. SANFORD-HARRIS is dean of students at Bunker Hill Community College, Boston, Massachusetts. She recently served as secretary of the National Academic Advising Association (1990–1992).

*Effective multicultural advising requires an awareness and acknowledgment of cultural differences and a sensitivity to various individual biases.*

# Advising Multicultural Populations for Achievement and Success

*Thomas Brown, Mario Rivas*

In *Guess Who's Coming to College: Your Students in 1990,* Harold Hodgkinson (1983) suggested that American colleges and universities were systematically ignoring the rapidly increasing percentage of minorities in the U.S. population. He went on to charge that higher education structures had been weak in planning for future generations of college students, who would increasingly be Asian, black, Hispanic, and Native American (persons of color and ethnic minorities).

In our society, general trends influence local action, and the trends are clear. By the year 2000, one-third of the nation's population will be composed of persons of color (American Council on Education, 1988). Green (1989, p. 3) has cited data indicating that 55 percent of Hispanic and almost 43 percent of black students are enrolled in two-year colleges, and public two-year colleges enroll more minority students than all public four-year colleges and universities combined (Astin, 1985). Few of these students ever go on to graduate from four-year institutions (Green, 1989). The community colleges are clearly the institutions of choice for increasing numbers of Asian, black, Hispanic, and Native American students. Thus, this sector of academe has a major leadership role to assume in order to meet the challenges of helping students of color enter and succeed in higher education.

As demonstrated in Zwerling (1986), community colleges have not done a good job of helping ethnic minority students achieve their goals, whether these are to transfer to four-year institutions or to complete vocational programs or associate degrees. Related to this poor performance is the fact that the likelihood of a student attaining the bachelor of arts degree

New Directions for Community Colleges, no. 82, Summer 1993 © Jossey-Bass Publishers is reduced significantly if the student begins postsecondary education in a community college (Astin, 1977, 1982; Breneman and Nelson, 1981). More often than not, the student fails to get sufficiently involved in the academic experience. Astin (1985) has identified involvement—or becoming connected to their education institutions—as the key to students' persistence.

Astin (1985) and Crockett (1985) are among those who have identified academic advising and academic advisers as the key links between students, curricula, and colleges. No single student service is mentioned more in retention research as an effective means of promoting student retention and success than academic advising (Thomas, 1990). However, the recognition of the importance of academic advising is tempered by the fact that student ratings of the usefulness of advising services are among the lowest in postsecondary education (Boyer, 1987; Astin, 1985).

With regard to ethnic minorities, community college advisers are on the front lines of American higher education. Advisers are key sources of information, guidance, and support for students. It is important, therefore, that they be fully aware of the challenges that confront them as they seek to respond effectively to the educational needs of an increasingly diverse student population. In this chapter, we identify some of the critical issues and appropriate responses for advisers who work with multicultural populations.

## Challenges in Developmental Advising

In considering the goal of becoming effective multicultural and pluralistic professionals, advisers should commit themselves to a developmental approach to advising (Ender, Winston, and Miller, 1984) and examine how this approach may be adversely affected when they interact with students from diverse cultural and ethnic backgrounds. The challenges confronting advisers who work with ethnic minorities are varied and complex; however, two in particular are especially important. First, advisers must develop an awareness of the diversity of cultural experiences in American society and how these affect advising relationships. This awareness is fundamental to the task of establishing rapport with students of color so as to facilitate their full involvement in the academic enterprise. Second, advisers must help ethnic minority students increase their levels of competence and achievement so that they can realize the anticipated benefits of a college education. A theme underlying both of these challenges is that advisers must adjust advising methodologies and strategies to accommodate the need of many students of color for more directive, concrete, tangible responses to their immediate problems.

**Responding to Cultural Differences.** Historically, intercultural relationships in the United States could be described as bilateral, involving whites and blacks, Anglos and Latinos, or whites and Asians. The new demographic realities have resulted in relationships that are multilateral and multilayered (Der, 1990). It is incumbent on all advisers, whatever their ethnicity, to develop and expand the knowledge and skills needed to interact effectively with increasingly diverse student populations. The responsibility for helping Asian, black, Hispanic, and Native American students cannot fall only on Asian, black, Hispanic, and Native American advisers; all students need mentors who are personally interested in their achievement, but these mentors do not necessarily have to share their ethnicity.

**Values Conflicts in Advising.** For advisers to succeed in cross-cultural advising interactions, they must become knowledgeable about how diversity is expressed in advising and how cultural differences between the adviser and the student can undermine the advising encounter. Furthermore, advisers must attain the levels of sensitivity, concern, and ability needed to address the developmental issues that students of color bring with them to college, issues ranging from emerging pride in their ethnic identities to the potentially paralyzing effects of societal racism and discrimination. This latter point is important because students' personal development has a direct impact on their readiness to pursue academic and intellectual goals (Schein, Laff, and Allen, 1987).

Much has been written about how cultural differences can undermine communication (Sue and Sue, 1990; Pederson, Darguns, Lonner, and Trimble, 1981; LeVine and Padilla, 1980; Tannen, 1990). Specifically, Sue and Sue (1990) have identified sources of conflict and misinterpretations in counseling interactions when there are differences in the cultural backgrounds of the counselor and counselee. Much in Sue and Sue's model applies to the work of academic advisers. Indeed, many of the examples that they use, as well as others in the counseling literature, describe academic advising situations.

Sue and Sue (1990) have described a number of generic characteristics of counseling, among which are the following: (1) Participants use standard English, (2) participants emphasize verbal communication, (3) participants focus on long-range goals, (4) the processes are often ambiguous and open to interpretation, (5) interactions are based on openness and the willingness of the client to share personal or intimate information with the counselor, and (6) the process focuses on the needs of the individual. They also have described third world group variables that relate to the counseling of Asians, blacks, Hispanics, and Native Americans. These variables differ from the generic characteristics of counseling, which are associated with white middle-class values, in that (1) standard English may be the second language, (2) the client is action-oriented and focuses on immediate, short-range, "present-time" goals, (3) the client requires a more concrete, structured, tangible approach, and (4) the client's interests are likely to be family-centered, group-oriented, based on cooperative not competitive individualism, or a combination thereof. Due to cultural differences, advisers must be aware of potential incongruencies in the communication process when advising ethnically diverse students because these differences often lead to miscommunication, misunderstanding, and a lack of engagement.

On the whole, people of color are likely to have had limited experiences with counseling or advising interactions (Vontress, 1981; Sue and Sue, 1990). Therefore, when engaged in cross-cultural communication, advisers "should be especially aware that the assumption that there is a common ground of shared expectancies is probably incorrect" (Yuen and Tinsley, 1981, p. 69). Among the generic characteristics of counseling is the expectation that interactions will be based on openness and the willingness of the client (advisee) to share personal and intimate information with the counselor (adviser). For Asians and Hispanics, however, discussion of personal issues beyond the boundaries of the family or community can be perceived as a betrayal of those to whom they are accustomed to turning for advice, support, and assistance.

Past experiences with racism and prejudice cause many people of color to be distrustful of persons from different backgrounds. In advising, this mistrust often produces hesitancy to disclose personal information. The experiences of these individuals may suggest that bureaucracies and their agents, in this instance, academic advisers, do not have their best interests at heart and are seeking to frustrate their goal achievement rather than support and advance it. These students may have concerns about being misunderstood, hurt, or taken advantage of if personal information is disclosed. When one has had a history of strained relations with the Bureau of Indian Affairs, United States Health and Human Services, Immigration and Naturalization, or any number of other bureaucratic agencies and their representatives, it is reasonable to expect reluctance to participate openly in an advising encounter.

It is essential for advisers to structure advising sessions to clarify the purposes, goals, and methods of academic advising so as to reduce advisee hesitancy. For example, the adviser should begin by inquiring about the student's prior advising experiences and his or her level of satisfaction therewith. If the adviser gleans that the student is unfamiliar with advising, then the appropriate response is to define advising, academic planning, and the decision-making process, outline roles and responsibilities, and discuss what may be gained from talking about issues and problems. It is particularly important to set forth the confidential nature of advising and the fact that nothing can legally be shared with anyone, inside or outside the institution, without the express consent of the advisee.

Another characteristic of advising that may be in conflict with the cultural experiences of many students of color is its nondirectiveness. An egalitarian presumption underlying advising calls for the adviser to set forth a range of alternatives, whereby the advisee makes the final decision about an appropriate course of action. This perspective is often at odds with role relationship experiences that stress hierarchical patterns of interaction and deference to authority.

Many students of color come from family situations where roles are well defined and expectations are clear. For example, Vietnamese children are taught from an early age to listen to authority figures and speak only when asked to do so. Advice, questions, and opinions are not encouraged (Do, 1983). Likewise, Attneave (1982) has observed that in most American Indian and Alaskan native social settings the dominant person is expected to be active and the subordinate person shows respect by quiet attentiveness. Similar dynamics of interaction with authority figures have also been observed for Latinos (Bernal and Flores-Ortiz, 1982), rural blacks (Vontress, 1981), and Puerto Ricans (Garcia-Preto, 1982). In a study of counseling style preferences, Exum and Lau (1988) found that Chinese students rated the directive approach more positively than the nondirective style. Similarly, Ruiz and Casas (1981) highlighted the importance of using a directive approach when engaging Chicano college students. The unwillingness of the adviser to accept a directive role may be unsettling to many students of color and leave them confused, disoriented, and dissatisfied with the advising encounter, which may in part account for the underutilization of student personnel services by students of color.

In setting forth third world group variables for counseling, Sue and Sue (1990) identified the need of many people of color for concrete, tangible, structured approaches to addressing and resolving issues and problems. Many students of color see advisers as "experts" (that is, authority figures) who have the "right" answers and "know" what students should do. The nondirective principle that underlies current advising practices may not prove satisfying to these students.

Terry O'Banion, a leading advocate of developmental advising and innovation in the community college sector, has asked, "Aren't there times when advisors know what is best for students, and when they do, don't they have a responsibility to share insights and experiences with students?" (O'Banion, 1987). Effective multicultural advising often requires advisers to adjust their advising strategies to accommodate the need of students of color for concrete, tangible responses in advising. This adjustment may be particularly important in early advising interactions, when students most expect advisers to provide them with clear direction.

**Diversity Within Diversity.** Allen Ivey (1981), former president of the American Psychological Association Division of Counseling Psychology, has argued that it is unethical to counsel a person with a cultural background different from one's own without appropriate information and sensitivity. It is also inappropriate to generalize broad knowledge about a cultural group to all individual group members. In this regard, Falicov (1982) has advised that broad cultural generalizations often do not do justice to regional, generational, socioeconomic, and other differences within specific ethnic groups.

Advising needs will differ based on the individual backgrounds and experiences of the students. For instance, who is the "Hispanic" being advised? Is she a first-generation Mexican American from a rural background, a recent arrival from Puerto Rico, or a fourth-generation Cuban American? Is the "Asian American" seated in the adviser's office a Vietnamese who fled to the United States at the time of the American withdrawal from Saigon, or has his Hmong family been lingering in the refugee camps of Bangkok for the past decade awaiting permission to emigrate? Is the "Native American" a product of a suburban experience, or has she lived her entire life on a reservation? Is the "African American" student the first in his family to go to college, a Haitian refugee, or the product of an affluent professional family? Sue and Sue (1990) have cautioned us not to generalize from generic cultural variables to all individuals within the groups with whom we work. Effective cross-cultural advisers must be aware of diversity within diversity. It is important, therefore, to make distinctions based on socioeconomic class, educational background, family structure, gender, and previous experiences with academic advising.

**Issues of Identity Development and Worldview.** The key to effective advising is communication; that is, both the adviser and advisee must be on the same wavelength if "contact" is to occur. With regard to effective communication with students of color, advisers should have an understanding of how students' social development can affect their ability to interact with an adviser of a different sociocultural background. Ibrahim (1985) observed that it is important to understand the cultural values and worldviews of students if we are to understand the culturally different client. Sue and Sue (1990), in turn, noted that the worldviews of minorities in the United States are shaped by racism and the subordinate position assigned to them in society. Advisers cannot work with black students (and other students of color) in a meaningful and effective manner unless they understand the philosophical assumptions and life experiences of these students (McEwen, Roper, Bryant, and Langa, 1990).

Wright (1987, p. 10) has charged that "current models of student development fail to account for the influence of culture on the developmental process and result in a fundamental lack of understanding of minority students." There are a number of ethnic identity models that have been developed, and these can help advisers to better understand and effectively respond to students of color (Atkinson, Morten, and Sue, 1983; Cross, 1971; Ruiz, 1990). These models all clarify the impact that socialization in a hostile environment can have on the identity development of persons of color. These identity models point out that there are passages or stages through which ethnic minorities move in developing a strong sense and acceptance of self and others.

A basic theme of the ethnic minority identity models is that students go through a developmental "immersion" stage wherein they are less likely to be receptive to communication with those outside their own ethnic group. This stage is generally followed by a transitional phase, which leads to an internalization or resolution phase where the person of color is self-appreciating, group appreciating, and selectively appreciating of others (Atkinson, Morten, and Sue, 1983). There is considerable research showing that students of color often prefer working with helping professionals who share their ethnicity. Sanchez and Atkinson (1983) found this to be the case for Mexican American students, and Johnson and Lashley (1989) collected similar data on Native American students. Pomales, Claiborn, and LaFramboise (1986) observed that black students see a "culturally sensitive" counselor as more competent than a "culturally blind" counselor.

The effective multicultural adviser must be willing to respect and support the social identity development of students of color. For example, this approach may mean not responding defensively to a black student who is in the angry immersion stage of development (Cross, 1971) and who may display overt hostility and resistance to the most culturally sensitive professional of different ethnicity. Steele (1990) has noted that to be black in America is to be a member of this nation's most despised and denigrated group. Advisers must recognize that many students of color have been expected to learn and develop in hostile environments (Wright, 1987). A single positive encounter with an aware adviser could be the catalyst that facilitates student development toward internalization of self-acceptance and full engagement in the academic enterprise.

It is also essential for advisers to self-appraise their own identity development within a pluralistic society in order to fully understand the concept of individual perceptions of reality (worldviews) associated with models of minority identity development. Ponterotto (1988, p. 147), citing Wrenn (1985), has asked, "What pragmatic use will a counselor's understanding of the client's racial consciousness level foster, if the counselor himself/herself is racially 'unconscious' and culturally encapsulated?" For example, an Asian American or Hispanic adviser should reflect on her or his own ethnicity, vis-à-vis ethnic identity development, to be aware of potential emotional conflicts that could hinder effective communication with students of color. Specific to white advisers, who comprise the greater number of advising professionals, there are white identity models that can help these individuals explore their own ethnicity as whites in U.S. society in order to bring to the surface emotional and attitudinal obstacles to effective communication. Katz and Ivey (1977) have charged that a failure to include opportunities for white professionals to address their own ethnic identities allows them the luxury of denying any responsibility for or connection with the racist system that oppresses the multicultural clients whom advisers are seeking to assist. The existing white identity models

(Ponterotto, 1988; Helms, 1984; Corvin and Wiggins, 1989) clarify the impact of being socialized as a member of the dominant group in American society and how this adversely influences effective communication with multicultural populations. These identity models propose passages or stages that whites go through in developing a sense of themselves as members of a pluralistic society.

A basic theme of these models is that whites experience a zealot-defensive (Ponterotto, 1988)/resistance (Corvin and Wiggins, 1989) stage and an integration/internalization stage in the transition to becoming effective multicultural persons. Corvin and Wiggins indicate that the internalization stage is characterized by integration of racial identity into personal identity, elimination of oppressive and exploitative attitudes and behaviors, internalization of a multicultural perspective, and orientation toward being a change agent.

Although we all may wish for an America in which people are judged by the content of their character, the reality is that experiences of racism and prejudice shape many perceptions and attitudes. As professionals, all advisers must be willing to face this reality and act to have a positive impact on individuals and systems.

### Beyond Engagement: Promoting Academic Achievement and Success

In his remarks to the American Council of Education conference Educating One-Third of a Nation, Alfredo de los Santos (1989), vice chancellor of the Maricopa Community College (Tempe, Arizona), pointed out that in the 1960s and 1970s the issues for students of color related to increased access to higher education opportunities; in the 1970s and 1980s education institutions turned their attention to retention; and for the 1990s the issues for students of color concern achievement of excellence and success. While access and retention remain important issues, advisers must challenge ethnic minority students to strive to higher levels of competence and achievement. Asian, black, brown, and Native American students must be encouraged to see education as a social responsibility to themselves and to their communities, and to our nation (Wright, 1987), a responsibility that calls for individual discipline and strength of purpose. Jaime Escalante, whose story was told in the film Stand and Deliver, inspires and motivates his students by telling them, "Success is a victory. It is a big bonus to your community and to your last name." The Escalante equation is "determination plus discipline plus hard work equals success."

Often, students of color come to college with low self-esteem and low self-confidence due to their prior experiences in education. Academic advisers can play an important role in helping these students set high goals for themselves and develop strategies to reach those goals. Advisers need to become knowledgeable and skillful about interventions that promote the academic achievement of students of color.

## Possible Interventions for Students of Color

Rivas (1990) has developed a task-focused academic advising model, the 0–100 percent method, that takes into account the social-psychological development of students of color and, specifically, how negative developmental experiences in education can undermine the student's ability to work hard, persist, and succeed in college. Central to this approach is the message that the student must focus on the task of developing competence (White, 1959) in college and in satisfying the human "need to know" (Maslow, 1968). The method uses the following six steps to provide the adviser and the student with a structure to organize and approach the challenges of college: (1) Review the student's academic record and learning history, looking for strengths and insights, weaknesses and lack of insights. (2) Define the student's personal, education, and career goals and related skills that must be developed to achieve desired goals. (3) In a nonthreatening way (using the interpersonal approaches already discussed in this chapter), assess the student's initial skill level (0–100 percent) in those areas identified as essential to achievement. (4) Establish standards of excellence (0–100 percent) that the student will work toward in each of the identified skill areas. (5) Identify curricular, cocurricular, and community learning experiences that will help the student develop skills and achieve desired goals. And (6) as part of an ongoing advising relationship, the student and adviser review and evaluate progress toward goal achievement and skill development.

Rivas uses a 0 to 100 scale, with 0 as "no skill" and 100 as "perfection." This approach is perceived by students as an understandable and straightforward way in which to assess their readiness for college. There are two important requisites, however, that the adviser should consider when using this approach: (1) Be straightforward about the need for the student to realistically appraise his or her skill level vis-à-vis the demands of college and future careers and (2) effectively communicate a sincere commitment to advise and support the student's work toward skill development. Because this process can be threatening, the student is encouraged to focus on the task of becoming skillful (task-involved) as opposed to comparing self to real or imagined "others" in a particular group (ego-involved) (Nicholls, 1984). Comparisons of self to others, especially when skills are low, can lead to feelings of shame, doubt, hopelessness, or helplessness. These negative feelings can undermine efforts to develop competence (Weiner, 1985).

Once the student has realistically appraised his or her skill levels, the adviser helps the student plan an academic program to achieve desired competence levels. For example, a student who is ill at ease participating in class or speaking in public could take a speech course to learn how to organize presentations, to be more comfortable talking before a group, or to effectively support an argument with details and acts. In the process of taking classes, the adviser and student are able to verify the student's initial self-appraisal and make appropriate changes in the student's academic program. For example, a student who rated herself a 40 in oral communication might discover that she has strengths that can lead to a higher skill rating (possibly 60) because she has excellent stage presence; but to effectively make that stage presence work, she needs to improve on her level of preparation, research, and practice before making a presentation.

Levin and Levin (1991) reviewed research and intervention programs for at-risk minority college students and offered suggestions for effective interventions. Although many of the suggestions did not come directly from adviser efforts, some of the approaches are potentially adaptable by advisers in their work with students of color. One of the major findings of the Levin and Levin study, which supports the work of Astin (1985), is that "quality interaction with faculty seems to be more important than any other single college factor in determining minority student persistence" (1991, p. 324). With regard to skills that students need to develop in college, advisers need to discover ways to facilitate ethnic minority students' quality interaction with faculty. A caveat here is that efforts in this direction must extend beyond simple referral of students to faculty. Advisers must acquaint students of color with the importance of interacting with professors and teach these students to communicate and interact effectively and successfully with faculty. Furthermore, advisers must work closely with faculty to develop structured mentor programs that produce quality interaction between students and faculty.

Levin and Levin (1991) also found that stand-alone study skills courses are not as effective as study skills courses that are connected to academic classes. Since the advising function of community college advisers often extends to teaching study skills modules, advisers should work closely with faculty to develop adjunct learning skills courses that better promote student skill building. A model program in this area is the Puente Project in Sacramento, California (Lachica and Sherwood, 1989). Under the auspices of the California Community College System, advisers undertake motivational and behavioral skills advising with students who want to improve their writing competence.

A third finding of the Levin and Levin (1991) study applicable to the work of advisers is that peer group methods are especially useful in promoting academic success. A similar conclusion was drawn by Pincus and DeCamp (1989) in a study of community college students. Grites (1984) stated that the group approach highlights the commonality of student concerns and that group advising is an effective alternative approach. Peer group interventions are an area in which advisers can promote educationally focused peer group interactions (Rivas, 1988). Such interactions are fundamental to increased academic and social integration and therefore merit consideration by advisers in their work with students of color.

## Conclusion

The effective multicultural and pluralistic adviser is aware of cultural differences and is sensitive to his or her own biases. Such an individual seeks to understand the bases of differences and recognizes that differences among people do not constitute a negative thing but rather a reality of the human experience. Such an adviser commits herself or himself to an understanding of differences and moves toward becoming a multicultural person. The effective multicultural, pluralistic adviser must examine personal attitudes and beliefs. This adviser recognizes the need to increase knowledge and information about the groups with whom he or she interacts. An adviser cannot expect to wake up one morning with pluralistic sensitivities; this goal requires effort (reading, interacting, and sharing with colleagues of color who have pluralistic backgrounds and experiences). Finally, in order to be effective cross-cultural and pluralistic professionals, advisers must look at their repertoires of advising skills and apply innovative strategies to support the success of increasingly diverse student populations.

Academic advisers are the key links between students of color and higher education. When advisers are culturally sensitive, willing to go the extra mile in support of students and to challenge students to excel rather than merely persist, and give students concrete, tangible strategies to take responsibility for their own learning and achievement, they can make a difference for these students, for their institutions, and for society.

## References

American Council on Education. *Educating One-Third of a Nation: The Conference Report.* Washington, D.C.: American Council on Education, 1988.

Astin, A. W. *Four Critical Years: Effects of College on Beliefs, Attitudes, and Knowledge.* San Francisco: Jossey-Bass, 1977.

Astin, A. W. *Minorities in American Higher Education: Recent Trends, Current Prospects, and Recommendations.* San Francisco: Jossey-Bass, 1982.

Astin, A. W. *Achieving Educational Excellence: A Critical Assessment of Priorities and Practices in Higher Education.* San Francisco: Jossey-Bass, 1985.

Atkinson, D. R., Morten, G., and Sue, D. W. *Counseling American Minorities: A Cross-Cultural Perspective.* Dubuque, Iowa: Brown, 1983.

Attneave, C. "American Indians and Alaska Native Families: Immigrants in Their Own Homeland." In M. McGoldrick, J. K. Pearce, and J. Giordano (eds.), *Ethnicity and Family Therapy.* New York: Guilford, 1982.

Bernal, G., and Flores-Ortiz, Y. "Latino Families in Therapy: Engagement and Evaluation." *Journal of Marital and Family Therapy*, 1982, 8 (3), 357–365.

Boyer, E. L. *College: The Undergraduate Experience in America.* New York: HarperCollins, 1987. 328 pp. (ED 279 259)

Breneman, D., and Nelson, S. *Financing Community Colleges.* Washington, D.C.: Brookings Institution, 1981.

Corvin, S. A., and Wiggins, F. "An Antiracism Training Model for White Professionals." *Journal of Multicultural Counseling and Development,* 1989, 17 (3), 105–114.

Crockett, D. S. "Academic Advising." In L. Noel, R. Levitz, D. Saluri, and Associates, *Increasing Student Retention: Effective Programs and Practices for Reducing the Dropout Rate.* San Francisco: Jossey-Bass, 1985.

Cross, W. E., Jr. "The Negro-to-Black Conversion Experience." *Black World,* 1971, 20 (9), 13–27.

de los Santos, A., Jr. "Setting Your Institutional Agenda." Paper presented at the American Council on Education conference Educating One-Third of a Nation, San Francisco, Nov. 1989.

Der, H. "Building Our Future Through Diversity." Paper presented at the Bay Area Library and Information Systems conference Developing Library Collections for California's Emerging Majority, San Francisco, Sept. 1990.

Do, V. T. "Cultural Differences: Implications in the Education of Vietnamese Students in U.S. Schools." In V. A. Smith and M. B. Dixon (eds.), *Second Lives: The Contemporary Immigrant/ Refugee Experience in Orange County.* Costa Mesa, Calif.: South Coast Repertory, 1983.

Ender, S. C., Winston, R. B., Jr., and Miller, T. K. "Academic Advising Reconsidered." In R. B. Winston, Jr., and others, *Developmental Academic Advising: Assessing Students' Educational, Career, and Personal Needs.* San Francisco: Jossey-Bass, 1984.

Exum, H. A., and Lau, E. Y. "Counseling Style Preference of Chinese College Students." *Journal of Multicultural Counseling and Development,* 1988, 16 (2), 84–92.

Falicov, C. "Mexican Families." In M. McGoldrick, J. K. Pearce, and J. Giordano (eds.), *Ethnicity and Family Therapy.* New York: Guilford, 1982.

Garcia-Preto, N. "Puerto Rican Families." In M. McGoldrick, J. K. Pearce, and J. Giordano (eds.), *Ethnicity and Family Therapy.* New York: Guilford, 1982.

Green, M. F. (ed.). *Minorities on Campus: A Handbook for Enhancing Diversity.* Washington, D.C.: American Council on Education, 1989.

Grites, T. J. "Techniques and Tools for Improving Advising." In R. B. Winston, Jr., and others, *Developmental Academic Advising: Assessing Students' Educational, Career, and Personal Needs.* San Francisco: Jossey-Bass, 1984.

Helms, J. E. "Toward a Theoretical Explanation of the Effects of Race on Counseling: A Black and White Model." *Counseling Psychologist,* 1984, 12 (4), 153–165.

Hodgkinson, H. L. *Guess Who's Coming to College: Your Students in 1990.* Washington, D.C.: National Institute of Independent Colleges and Universities, 1983. 22 pp. (ED 225 497)

Ibrahim, F. A. "Effective Cross-Cultural Counseling and Psychotherapy: A Framework." *Counseling Psychologist,* 1985, 3, 625–638.

Ivey, A. "Foreword." In D. W. Sue, *Counseling the Culturally Different: Theory and Practice.* New York: Wiley, 1981.

Johnson, M. E., and Lashley, K. H. "Influence of Native Americans' Cultural Commitment on Preferences for Counselor Ethnicity and Expectations About Counseling." *Journal of Multicultural Counseling and Development,* 1989, 17 (3), 115–122.

Katz, J. H., and Ivey, A. "White Awareness: The Frontier of Racism Awareness Training." *Personnel and Guidance Journal,* 1977, 55 (8), 485–489.

Lachica, J., and Sherwood, W. *Sacramento City College Five Year Follow-up Study of Puente Students.* Berkeley: Office of the President, University of California, 1989.

Levin, M. E., and Levin, J. R. "A Critical Examination of Academic Retention Programs for At-Risk Minority College Students." *Journal of College Student Development,* 1991, 32 (4), 323–334.

LeVine, E. S., and Padilla, A. M. *Crossing Cultures in Therapy: Pluralistic Counseling for the Hispanic.* Monterey, Calif.: Brooks/Cole, 1980.

McEwen, M. K., Roper, L. D., Bryant, D. R., and Langa, M. J. "Incorporating the Development of African-American Students into Psychosocial Theories of Student Development." *Journal of College Student Development,* 1990, *31* (5), 429–436.

Maslow, A. H. *Toward a Psychology of Being.* Princeton, N.J.: Van Nostrand Reinhold, 1968.

Nicholls, J. G. "Achievement Motivation: Conceptions of Ability, Subjective Experience, Task Choice, and Performance." *Psychological Review,* 1984, *91* (3), 328–346.

O'Banion, T. "Increasing Diversity and the Challenge to Academic Advising." Paper presented at the annual meeting of the National Academic Advising Association, Chicago, Oct. 1987.

Pederson, P., Darguns, J., Lonner, W., and Trimble, J. (eds.). *Counseling Across Cultures.* Honolulu: University of Hawaii Press, 1981.

Pincus, F. L., and DeCamp, S. "Minority Community College Students Who Transfer to Four-Year Colleges: A Study of a Matched Sample of B.A. Recipients and Non-Recipients." *Community and Junior College Quarterly of Research and Practice,* 1989, *13* (3–4), 191–219.

Pomales, J., Claiborn, C. D., and LaFramboise, T. D. "Effects of Black Students' Racial Identity on Perceptions of White Counselors Varying in Cultural Sensitivity." *Journal of Counseling Psychology,* 1986, *33* (1), 57–61.

Ponterotto, J. G. "Racial Consciousness Development Among White Counselor Trainees: A Stage Model." *Journal of Multicultural Counseling and Development,* 1988, *16* (4), 146–156.

Rivas, M. "An Exploratory Study of a Group Intervention for Underprepared Ethnic Minority Students Entering College." Unpublished doctoral dissertation, Counseling and Student Personnel Psychology Program, University of Minnesota, 1988.

Rivas, M. "Zero to 100 Percent Advising Method: A Task-Focused Academic Advising Model to Empower Students to Take Responsibility for Their Own Learning, Achievement and Success." Paper presented at the annual meeting of the National Academic Advising Association, Anaheim, California, Oct. 1990.

Ruiz, A. S. "Ethnic Identity: Crisis and Resolution." *Journal of Multicultural Counseling and Development,* 1990, *18* (1), 29–40.

Ruiz, R., and Casas, J. "Culturally Relevant and Behavioristic Counseling for Chicano College Students." In P. Pederson, J. Darguns, W. Lonner, and J. Trimble (eds.), *Counseling Across Cultures.* Honolulu: University of Hawaii Press, 1981.

Sanchez, A. R., and Atkinson, D. R. "Mexican-American Cultural Commitment, Preference for Counselor Ethnicity, and Willingness to Use Counseling." *Journal of Counseling Psychology,* 1983, *30* (2), 215–220.

Schein, H. K., Laff, N. S., and Allen, D. R. *Giving Advice to Students: A Road Map for College Professionals.* American College Personnel Association Media Publications, no. 44. Alexandria, Va.: American College Personnel Association, 1987. 146 pp. (ED 324 622)

Steele, S. *The Content of Our Character: A New Vision of Race in America.* New York: St. Martin's Press, 1990.

Sue, D. W., and Sue, D. *Counseling the Culturally Different: Theory and Practice.* (2nd ed.) New York: Wiley, 1990.

Tannen, D. *You Just Don't Understand.* New York: Ballantine Books, 1990.

Thomas, R. O. "Programs and Activities for Improved Retention." In D. Hossler, J. P. Bean, and Associates, *The Strategic Management of College Enrollments.* San Francisco: Jossey-Bass, 1990.

Vontress, C. "Racial and Ethnic Barriers in Counseling." In P. Pederson, J. Darguns, W. Lonner, and J. Trimble (eds.), *Counseling Across Cultures.* Honolulu: University of Hawaii Press, 1981.

Weiner, B. "An Attributional Theory of Achievement Motivation and Emotion." *Psychological Review,* 1985, *92* (4), 548–573.

White, R. W. "Motivation Reconsidered: The Concept of Competence." *Psychological Review,* 1959, *66* (5), 297–333.

Wrenn, C. G. "Afterward: The Culturally Encapsulated Counselor Revisited." In P. Peterson (ed.), *Handbook of Cross-Cultural Counseling and Therapy*. Westport, Conn.: Greenwood Press, 1985.

Wright, D. J. (ed.). *Responding to the Needs of Today's Minority Students*. New Directions for Student Services, no. 38. San Francisco: Jossey-Bass, 1987.

Yuen, R.K.W., and Tinsley, H.E.A. "International and American Students' Expectancies About Counseling." *Journal of Counseling Psychology*, 1981, 28 (1), 66–69.

Zwerling, L. S. (ed.). *The Community College and Its Critics*. New Directions for Community Colleges, no. 54. San Francisco: Jossey-Bass, 1986.

*THOMAS BROWN is dean of Advising Services and Special Programs at Saint Mary's College of California. He is a past member of the board of directors of the National Academic Advising Association.*

*MARIO RIVAS is director of the Advising Center and Learning Assistance Center at San Francisco State University.*

*Effective academic advising programs require structured intervention*
*strategies at specified times from admission to graduation.*

# Intrusive Academic Advising

*Martha T. Garing*

Development of intrusive advising relationships requires structured strategies
of intervention by advisers at specified times throughout the students' semesters
in college. Although these strategies will differ depending on the institution's
size, organizational structure, and staffing model, it is critical that techniques are
implemented so that advising is perceived *and* delivered as intrusive, and
developmental, and serves as a catalyst for building personalized student-
adviser relationships. When these strategies are integrated as necessary components of the institution's advising system, not only are the efficiency and
effectiveness of advising enhanced, but the retention of students is ultimately
affected in a positive way due to the solidness of this critical student-adviser link.

Advising time can be divided into two major periods: inquiry to enrollment and enrollment to graduation. During the first period, students complete their admissions processes, participate in assessment activities, register
for classes, and receive orientation programming. The actual order of these
events may vary depending on the particular institutional system or structure. The second period of advising, enrollment to graduation, is crucial for
students and advisers in terms of implementation of intrusive interventions
and maximization of the effectiveness of advising. Special attention must be
given to first-semester freshmen, in particular; they require advising strategies that serve as checkpoints or "early-alert" techniques. These strategies
are modified after the first semester to the point of the students' departure or
graduation, taking into account the students' skills, needs, and course progress.

## Inquiry to Enrollment

During this first period, advising should play a key role and yet often is taken
for granted by advisers, or advisers may feel that they play only a peripheral

role. In many institutions, the admission, assessment, registration, and orientation processes are primarily administrative; advisers (particularly those who are faculty members) may not get directly involved in this first period of advising at all. The following is an outline of specific strategies for intrusive advising that advisers can implement during each stage of the first critical period of advising. (Adaptations obviously will need to be made, given variations in the degree to which advisers can or are able to be involved.)

**Admissions.** Prospective students are significantly influenced in their decision to attend a particular two-year institution by the institution's academic programs, level of faculty-student interaction, and types of academic resources or support services. As a result, students who receive adequate and accurate information at the point of admission are more likely to select that institution. Although the admissions personnel in most institutions handle these processes, advisers can assume an active role through involvement (as wanted or as necessary) in the interviewing process, perhaps through referrals from admissions for advising assistance with targeted student applicants such as those who are undecided or underprepared. This involvement of advisers can occur before, during, or after the admissions interview, for those institutions that utilize personal interviews. Advisers can also participate in the development of academic brochures, either on program-specific areas (degree programs) or on more general areas ("Advising services for undecided students at . . . "). This strategy may be most relevant in larger institutions where interviews are not utilized to a significant degree or where advisers have little involvement with the admissions process.

**Assessment.** Due to the increasingly diverse student populations who enroll at two-year colleges, it is important to provide assessment opportunities for all students in the areas of reading, writing, and mathematics. The results of this assessment are critical to the advising process, ensuring that students are enrolled in courses that match their skill and ability levels. Regardless of the type of assessment utilized (Assessment Skills for Successful Entry and Transfer, Educational Testing Service, in-house assessment tools) and the time and format in which the assessment is administered (during the summer, as part of an orientation program), advisers must become actively engaged in assessment.

Specifically, advisers, first, must receive assessment scores for all of their advisees; this is particularly important for advisers who may not conduct the initial advising sessions with their assigned advisees. Second, advisers must understand the implications of the assessment results for their advisees' intended programs of study. Third, they must communicate the institution's options regarding assessment to students who may not agree with the assessment results (for example, the opportunities, if any, for retaking the tests and whether placement is mandatory); this communication about options is particularly important for institutions that have required competencies in reading, writing, and mathematics. Fourth, advisers must sensitively address their advisees' questions and concerns about the assessment results; this sensitivity is critical when advisers must confront their students with the fact that the goal of building their skills through enrollment in remedial courses will require an additional semester or summer of coursework.

**Registration and Advising.** Although the actual process of registration is an administrative function, advisers should play a critical role by providing accurate information and by using the registration process as a time to establish the basis for all future adviser-advisee encounters. Amidst the variety of formats in which advising and registration occur (group summer sessions, telephone registration, centralized via registrar's office, decentralized via computers in advisers' offices), the adviser can play a critical role by (1) discussing the students' personal and career goals, their reasons for selecting their programs of study, and their knowledge of the demands of those particular programs; (2) providing students with their assessment scores and explaining what the impact will be on their first-semester course selections; (3) providing students with an overview of their academic programs, including a semester-by-semester suggested outline of courses; (4) outlining the expectations of the adviser-advisee relationship; and (5) providing students with pertinent information about office hours, location, and accessibility (appointment only, walk-in).

**Orientation.** Regardless of the orientation structure, format, and timing (summer, fall), it is important that the orientation experience include opportunities to acquaint students with basic collegiate information so that they can make informed decisions about their personal, social, academic, and career goals. Advisers should play an integral role in the orientation experience, since orientation is the initial critical time of advising new students.

Advisers can enhance their intrusive advising role by (1) arranging to meet personally (one-on-one or in small groups) with their advisees during orientation to begin building a relationship capable of answering typical advisee questions such as "Who am I?" "What do I want to do?" and "How can the institution help me get there?" (2) utilizing the orientation process to set the stage for fulfilling the three expectations that most advisees desire from their advisers: accessibility, specific and accurate information, and a personal and caring relationship; (3) participating in the institutional orientation program as a means of realistically implementing O'Banion's (1984) five stages of advising: exploration of life goals (values), exploration of education and career goals, selection of education program, selection of courses, and scheduling of classes; and (4) becoming involved in or at least knowledgeable about parent or family orientation programming, a critical component of intrusive advising given the degree to which parents, spouses, and families are getting involved with advising concerns and legal issues.

Advisers too frequently view orientation as an event that does not directly involve them, perhaps because advising, registration, and orientation are actually physically separate and segregated activities. However, intrusive advising demands that advisers begin viewing orientation as a means to an end and not as an end itself or as an event that is planned and executed solely by nonacademic personnel.

Sage Junior College in Albany, New York, where I serve as an associate dean of student development, has developed an integrative advising, registration, and orientation system in which advisers and advising play critical roles. The orientation program is a required two-day program for all freshmen and transfer students held in the fall prior to the start of classes. During the first day of the program, students participate in three workshop sessions in which they are introduced to one another, to skills in decision making, and to career exploration. Most advisers facilitate one of these workshop sessions, thus exemplifying the principle that advisers are an integral part of the college, both through their advising roles and as participating members of the college community.

On the second day of the program, all students participate in organized and personalized stages of a structured advising process: In Stage 1, all new students meet with staff in their respective academic divisions to receive program-specific information regarding their majors, degree requirements, academic terminology, and so on. (All program advisers are present at this division meeting.) In Stage 2, following the division meeting, students break into small groups with their assigned advisers to discuss their goals and their programs and to begin course scheduling. All students are also given advising appointments for later that day to meet personally with their advisers. In Stage 3, students meet one-on-one at their scheduled appointment times with their advisers to finalize their selections of courses. (These appointments are held in the gymnasium, where all of the other student services personnel are also located for the period of registration; this facilitates student access to advisers and to the appropriate administrative offices.) Finally, in Stage 4, students register for classes.

Sage Junior College has a faculty-based advising system in which most full-time faculty serve as advisers in their respective divisions. Intrusive advising has become a trademark of these advisers, and new students have rated their satisfaction with advising services at 85 percent or higher since 1984.

### Enrollment to Graduation

This second period of advising is the one with which advisers are most familiar and accepting of their various roles. Once students are enrolled in classes, advisers must initiate strategies or intrusive intervention techniques that provide necessary consistency for advisees, that serve as checkpoints or early-alert safeguards in the advising process, and that enhance the advising relationship in terms of assistance, problem solving, and guidance. There are four critical times for advising during which advisers should implement intrusive strategies for first-semester students.

**Three Weeks (First Critical Time).** Within the first three weeks of the semester, students have begun their adjustment processes, both academically and personally. They are feeling more comfortable about asking questions, they have met other students, they know what they like and do not like, and they have a clearer understanding of their course materials. As a result, adviser intervention is critical to determine students' satisfaction with their courses and majors, to proactively address any perceived problem areas, and to provide relevant information on campus services.

Strategies to accomplish a three-week intervention include the following: (1) Schedule a group meeting of first-semester advisees to informally address the issues of academic and personal adjustment and course and major satisfaction, as well as any other problem areas. If possible, select a meeting time when all students are available and offer refreshments to encourage a more informal discussion atmosphere. Second-year students (research assistants, student mentors, and student advisers) can serve as valuable assistants in these meetings to lessen anxiety, heighten peer credibility, and enhance, from a peer perspective, the importance of the group meeting. (2) Send a brief note, memo, or postcard to all first-semester advisees inviting them to stop by or make an appointment to discuss how their classes are going; include a business card with office location and hours. Although not all students will follow up, this type of intrusive outreach requires little additional effort from advisers, and it may make a critical difference in whether or not a student feels encouraged to ask for help. A variation of this technique is to mail an attractive departmental or informational newsletter to all advisees at the three-week point, including items such as a list of available academic support services (tutoring; mathematics, accounting, reading, or writing laboratories; self-help workshops) or an outline of on-campus career resources, advisers' office hours and locations, and library resources. Students who would not actively seek out such services on their own may take advantage of them after receiving a newsletter of this type.

**Six Weeks or Midterm (Second Critical Time).** By the sixth week of classes or at midterm, students have a concrete understanding of how they are doing in their classes; many will have had at least one major examination grade or project to indicate their academic progress thus far. Students will also have established a pattern of class attendance and homework completion, and they are usually able to identify which styles or types of classes are most or least beneficial to them. Their social adjustment outside of the classroom has probably either positively supplemented their academic progress or has begun to show signs of trouble.

Advisers need to take advantage of the six-week intervention to positively support their students' efforts and to provide guidance and direction where improvement is needed. Strategies include the following: (1) Utilize midterm grade reports to discuss academic trends and options; in some cases, students will need to be counseled about dropping a class, changing their major, and seeking tutorial assistance. (2) Set up personal appointments with students whose midterm progress reports clearly indicate that there will be difficulty in successfully completing the semester; it is important that advisers establish specific plans of action for these students, indicating that recovery may be possible but that immediate corrective measures must be taken. (3) Coordinate the mailing of midterm progress reports with the scheduling of a meeting (individual or group) with advisees; if students have to physically pick up their reports from their advisers, there is more of a built-in opportunity for intrusive advising. (4) Provide advisees with specific referral information and resources; materials may be routinely available (lists of tutors and their locations, career development materials, time management information, test-taking strategies) or may be various one-page listings especially prepared for midterm assistance. (5) Utilize any of the above intervention strategies as a means for also preparing students for preregistration; it is important that advisers reiterate to advisees what their responsibilities are (reviewing the upcoming semester's course offerings, tentatively plotting out a schedule, and the like).

**Preregistration (Third Critical Time).** Preregistration is not only a time for students to register for classes but also a critical point of decision making and clarification. By the time students are actually preregistering, they have clear indications of their academic progress during the current semester and are focusing more attention on the next semester. If progress is satisfactory, students will be considering the appropriate courses for the following semester and should be carefully reviewing their degree completion requirements with regard to summer plans, internship options and requirements, and the like. If progress is not satisfactory, if a student is confused over a choice of major, or if consideration is being given to not returning to college, students need to utilize the preregistration time for discussion and exploration.

Advisers should play a proactive role in preregistration and avoid the option of merely signing off on preregistration cards. Depending on the system for preregistration, intrusive intervention strategies include the following: (1) Meet personally with advisees to plan appropriate courses of action; if the six-week intervention strategy was successful, this meeting should, ideally, flow more smoothly, since the student comes to the preregistration meeting prepared (not with a blank form or with empty hands). (2) Encourage students to utilize the period of preregistration as a time to complete financial aid paperwork, investigate future independent study or internship possibilities, and reconsider work hours and priorities in view of the next semester's coursework. (3) Help undecided, confused, and at-risk students develop planning timetables; students in these categories should be encouraged to utilize appropriate referral sources and resources and then to follow up again within a specified time frame with their advisers. (4) Call or write the students who did not preregister or who failed to show for their preregistration appointments.

**Between Semesters (Fourth Critical Time).** Advisers may not be actively involved in any between-semester intervention strategies because much of what happens between semesters is usually thought of in terms of administrative functions (academic actions, dean's list). However, in many cases, students require more intrusive intervention after the semester has ended and after the grades have been received. Students tend to "disappear" more frequently between semesters, sometimes regardless of their academic standing, due to family pressures, changes in work, or perceived changes in career goals. Without the structure and support of the college setting, students may become isolated and lose sight of their planning or direction.

Advisers can enhance the linkages with their advisees between semesters through intervention techniques such as the following: (1) Apprise advisees who are placed on academic probation of their options and any academic restrictions; this can be done through personal interviews or through personalized notes. (2) Send letters or congratulations to advisees who make the dean's list. (3) Review the records of advisees who are dismissed to determine what, if any, patterns or warning signals exist that may be of assistance in future advising sessions. (4) Contact advisees who are not returning for the next semester; this can be done by telephone or by mail.

## Conclusion

Intrusive advising at four critical times during the first semester and three times each semester thereafter (six weeks, preregistration, and between semesters) provides long-term benefits for the advisers, the students, the adviser-student relationship, and, ultimately, for the institution. As a result of intrusive intervention strategies, advisers will have had direct, personal, and informative contact with their advisees a minimum of five times during the students' first semester (including orientation). This contact builds student-adviser trust and respect and student responsibility—all important elements of a positive advising relationship.

## Reference

O'Banion, T. "Integrating Academic Advising and Career Planning." In R. B. Winston, Jr., and others, *Developmental Academic Advising: Addressing Students' Educational, Career, and Personal Needs.* San Francisco: Jossey-Bass, 1984.

MARTHA T. GARING is associate dean of student development at Sage Junior College, Albany, New York. She is a former member of the board of the National Academic Advising Association.

*An annotated bibliography is provided on academic advising in community colleges. It includes sources concerned with the philosophy of advising, the organization of counseling programs and departments, advising personnel, and intrusive academic advising.*

# Sources and Additional Information: Academic Advising in the Community College

*Karin Petersen Hsiao*

Academic advising is a process designed to help students negotiate their coursework in college. Several questions that surround the activity come up repeatedly: Who should do the advising? Can it be put in reproducible format? Can it be made student accessible? Should it be intrusive or proactive? This section considers the way in which these questions are being treated in the literature.

The following source citations represent the most current literature in the ERIC data base on academic advising in community colleges. Most ERIC documents (references with "ED" numbers) can be read on microfiche at approximately nine hundred libraries worldwide. In addition, most can be ordered on microfiche or in paper copy from the ERIC Document Reproduction Service (EDRS) at 800-443-ERIC. Journal articles are not available from EDRS but can be acquired through regular library channels or purchased from the University Microfilms International Articles Clearinghouse at 800-521-0600, extension 533.

## General Sources

These sources present overviews of academic advising and the role of the academic adviser in the community college, and they describe various tools used by advising personnel in the performance of their jobs.

Carroll, B. W., and Tarasuk, P. E. "A New Vision for Student Development Services for the 90s." *Community College Review*, 1991, *19* (2), 32–42.

This article presents a comprehensive model of development guidance and counseling for community colleges. Carroll and Tarasuk review historical trends and recent changes in community college counseling, highlighting issues related to role confusion and changes in focus. They also describe various counselor roles and advising program components (namely, individual planning, guidance curriculum, responsive services, and program management).

Ford, J., and Ford, S. S. *Producing a Comprehensive Academic Advising Handbook.* Houston: Smith College and Student Academic Services, Houston Baptist University, 1991. 13 pp. (ED 339 435)

This comprehensive academic advising handbook is attractive, useful, versatile, and inexpensive. It is the cornerstone of a well-developed and well-implemented academic advising program. Seven steps that have proved effective in handbook development are discussed in this guide to handbook production. They include being committed to the project, determining the objectives and purposes of the handbook, and addressing appropriate topics. Handbook organization, typing and printing, and updating policies and procedures are discussed as well.

Matsen, M. E. "Computer Assisted Advising Tool (CAAT)." Paper presented at the 14th annual meeting of the League for Innovation in the Community College, San Francisco, October 1988. 21 pp. (ED 295 712)

Lane Community College's Computer Assisted Advising Tool (CAAT), which compares degree requirements with courses completed, is used by counselors to help students develop a plan for the completion of a degree or certificate. An online degree evaluation program compares a student's transcript, including waivers and course substitutions, with the stored requirements profile for a selected degree program. A report is then generated, listing all requirements and indicating which the student has completed and which remain unsatisfied. The CAAT report is arranged chronologically, providing the student and the counselor with a suggested schedule for completion of any given degree program from matriculation to graduation. Information on the CAAT files and sample reports are appended.

Pulliams, P. *The Emerging Role of the Community College Counselor. Highlights: An ERIC/CAPS Digest.* Ann Arbor, Mich.: ERIC Clearinghouse on Counseling and Personnel Services, 1990. 3 pp. (ED 315 707)

The increases in the numbers of adult, minority, women, part-time, and displaced students attending community colleges have caused a shift in the role of community college counselors from an in loco parentis emphasis on personal counseling, vocational guidance, and social support to new roles as student developers and learning agents. As student developers, counselors must communicate the importance of academic skill building and help students understand the value of their academic endeavors. As learning agents, counselors must assist, manage, and encourage students to build a pattern of success.

## Organization of Advising Programs

Academic advising programs in community colleges are organized in a variety of ways. These sources discuss the delivery mechanisms used for advising services at several different colleges.

Hadden, C. "The Placement Process at Colorado Mountain College: Placement Testing and the Advising Matrix." Paper presented at the conference Freshman Year Experience, Columbia, South Carolina, December 1988. 42 pp. (ED 302 298)

At Colorado Mountain College (CMC), academic advising is based on a comparison of students' basic skills with the skill requirements of individual courses. Students who enter CMC to obtain a degree must take placement tests in writing, reading, mathematics, and study skills before they can enroll in classes. An academic adviser uses placement test scores not only to advise students on the appropriate mathematics and composition classes but also to help students select all of their other classes.

Each term, instructors are surveyed regarding prerequisites, written work, tests, quizzes, homework, projects, oral work, experiments, textbooks, writing skills, reading skills, mathematics skills, and lecture styles. Their responses are entered into a data base program, and the resulting advising matrix can be printed out in either a short or long version. Attachments include testing and advising flowcharts, instructions for constructing an advising matrix, sample letters to instructors and an instructor questionnaire, copies of the long and short forms of the advising matrix, and information on determining the reading levels of textbooks.

Halpin, R. L. *A Study of Advisement Systems for Part-Time Students in SUNY Community Colleges.* Albany: Two-Year College Development Center, State University of New York, 1989. 32 pp. (ED 310 812)

In spring 1989, a study was conducted on the academic advising systems and practices in place for part-time students at twenty-seven State University of New York community colleges. The purpose of the study was to gather information on the advising systems and to determine if adult, part-time evening students had the same access to advising services as full-time day students.

Personal interviews were conducted with thirty faculty and staff members who were responsible for the academic advising of part-time students at the colleges. An analysis of responses revealed the following: (1) Few outreach programs were available for part-time students attending in the evening. (2) Students who attended classes at extension sites appeared to be better served as a result of the specific assignment of advising responsibilities to a site coordinator. (3) Many colleges had instituted evening advising centers to increase student-staff contact. And (4) in about one-half of the colleges, the administrative structure for the advising of full-time matriculated students was the same as for part-time matriculated students. The most common response to the question about needed improvements was "to have greater evening and weekend availability of advisement."

Railsback, G., and Colby, A. *Improving Academic Advising at the Community College: ERIC Digest.* Los Angeles: ERIC Clearinghouse for Junior Colleges, 1988. 6 pp. (ED 320 647)

While there is general consensus on the importance of good academic advising to student success and support for the American College Testing Program's developmental concept of advising, there is less agreement on the most effective model for delivery. Research suggests that both faculty-oriented advising and professional counselor-oriented systems have fallen short of their intended purposes.

Steps to improve academic advising include the following: (1) preparing, reviewing, and revising a written plan detailing the goals and functions of academic advising; (2) screening potential advisers and informing them that they must be willing to do more than help students schedule classes; (3) requiring that students meet on a regular basis with their advisers; (4) implementing advising programs in which counselors and teachers work together as a team; (5) rewarding the efforts of those involved in academic advising; (6) training advisers in basic counseling skills and techniques; (7) using computers in academic advising; and (8) assessing students and administrators to determine if the advising system is meeting its goals.

## Academic Advising Personnel

The sources in this section discuss the training and development of academic advising personnel, and counselor job satisfaction.

Coll, K. M., and House, R. M. "Empirical Implications for the Training and Professional Development of Community College Counselors." *Community College Review*, 1991, *19* (2), 43–52.

Coll and House describe a study of the appropriate major for and professional development needs of community college counselors, highlighting survey responses from counselor educators, student services co-workers, and Oregon community college counselors. They present findings concerning counselor duties and functions and perceptions of counselor role conflict and role ambiguity.

Coll, K., and Rice, R. "Job Satisfaction Among Community College Counselors." *Community and Junior College Quarterly of Research and Practice,* 1990, *14* (2), 83–91.

In this article, Coll and Rice describe a study of job satisfaction and factors influencing satisfaction among community college counselors in Oregon. They report general dissatisfaction with leadership and conclude that teaching load, job title, incompatible demands, unclear explanations, and conflicting resources all affect counselor satisfaction.

Harley, R., and McCabe, M. *Pima Community College Counselor's Handbook.* (Rev. ed.) Tucson, Ariz.: Pima Community College, 1990. 108 pp. (ED 338 291)

Developed for counselors at Pima Community College (PCC), this ten-part handbook provides information on counselor responsibilities, ethics, record keeping, assistance for students in distress, and diagnostic and referral procedures. Part One reviews the philosophy, general parameters, terminology, and goals of counseling and discusses selected statements of the Ethical Standards of the American Association for Counseling and Development. Part Two reviews issues and concepts relating to confidentiality. Part Three discusses record keeping and provides samples of various forms. Part Four examines the student code of conduct and the scholastic ethics code and discusses the use of the consulting and the counseling functions in therapy. Part Five discusses procedures for counseling students who have sexual harassment or discrimination complaints. Part Six discusses the relationship between the counselor with the campus police. Part Seven reviews referral procedures and community resources. Part Eight presents detailed information on counselor assistance to students in crisis or distress. Part Nine presents supplemental information, including charts on sexual harassment and the stages of suicide. And Part Ten provides references and a memorandum from PCC's attorney on the legal aspects of confidentiality.

### Intrusive Academic Advising

Increasingly, community college advisers and counselors are using intrusive advising techniques, intervening at specified times throughout students' careers. The following sources describe several such programs.

Onofrio, A., and others. *A Student Development Model for Academic Advising.* Cicero, Ill.: Morton College Counseling Center, 1988. 26 pp. (ED 300 095)

In spring 1985, the counseling staff at Morton College (MC) instituted a student development model for academic advising to encourage students to assume greater responsibility in planning their education and career goals. During their first academic advising appointment, new students are made aware of the importance of their commitment to their education goals and of existing course and program requirements. Career and life goals are discussed in relation to the students' chosen fields, and students needing help in identifying goals are referred to the Career Search Program and encouraged to begin career counseling. Students are also introduced to helpful MC resources, such as the counseling and academic skills centers, and specific recommendations for success are offered by counselors or advisers.

After the first advising session, students are encouraged to take responsibility for selecting and registering for their own courses, though assistance is available for those who continue to need help in planning their programs to meet college and career requirements. The advising model also makes provisions for alerting students who are not making satisfactory academic progress in their courses. Exhibits include informational materials given to students as part of the advising process and the advising program survey.

Belcher, M. J. *Costs Versus Benefits: An Evaluation of the Academic Alert System.* Research Report No. 91-02R. Miami: Florida Office of Institutional Research, Miami-Dade Community College, 1991. 45 pp. (ED 340 423)

At Miami-Dade Community College, the academic alert system informs students about their progress midway through a semester through the use of individualized letters based on faculty reports on student progress and attendance. In 1991, an evaluation of the alert system was undertaken to ascertain the benefits of the system and to determine the validity of the information that it provides. Study findings included the following: (1) Over two-thirds of the faculty and administrators thought that students would know where they stood at midterm without the alert system, as did one-third of the students. (2) Of the students who reported that their letters called for improvement in their performance, 80 percent said they had made changes to comply. (3) Seventy-two percent of the students reported that the information they received was accurate, and over 80 percent thought the information they received was helpful. (4) The largest group of faculty and administrators (40 percent) thought that only students in academic difficulty should receive letters. And (5) new students were more likely to rate academic alert information helpful than were returning students.

Jefcoat, H. G. "Advisement Intervention: A Key Strategy for a New Age— Student Consumerism." Paper presented at the annual meeting of the National Rural Education Association, Jackson, Mississippi, October 1991. 29 pp. (ED 340 546)

This paper describes the advisement intervention system at East Central Community College (ECCC) in Decatur, Mississippi, recognized by the Small/Rural Community College Commission as an "exemplary program."

The paper also provides suggestions for revising or developing an advising program.

The advising program at ECCC underwent changes—from a traditionalist to a consumerist orientation—to adequately meet the needs of and to become accountable to the fourteen hundred students that it serves. The program involved five advising intervention meetings scheduled throughout the year to address specific content and purposes, and a graduation transfer checklist was developed to actively involve students in the process of tracking their academic progress, particularly in the core courses required for graduation. In addition, an academic advising evaluation procedure and an effective adviser assignment method were developed. A better communication network was implemented, including early alert absentee notifications and academic progress mailings for students experiencing problems in these areas. Students are required to complete an advising checklist to identify problems or potential problems related to academics. An adviser sheet was also developed to promote goal setting, which fosters discussion between student and adviser.

## Other Resources

The National Academic Advising Association (NACADA) is a valuable resource for administrators and others who seek information about academic advising. Incorporated in 1979, with 429 members, NACADA's membership now numbers over 3,000 and includes faculty, professional advisers, administrators, counselors, and others interested in advising from across the United States and Canada.

To address critical issues in advising, NACADA publishes a journal and a newsletter, hosts one national and ten regional conferences annually, develops special publications and resource materials, and, in partnership with the American College Testing (ACT) Program, hosts the Summer Institute on Academic Advising and the ACT/NACADA Awards Program. Information about NACADA can be obtained from NACADA Executive Office, Kansas State University, 2323 Anderson Avenue, Manhattan, KS 66502.

*KARIN PETERSEN HSIAO is a research librarian and former user services coordinator at the ERIC Clearinghouse for Junior Colleges.*

# INDEX

Academic advisers: groups of majors and, 80; intrusive advising by, 97–103
Academic advising: definition of, 9; organizational models, 34–35; policy statements, 36, 43; student retention and, 22, 26–28, 60, 84; student transfer completion and, 28–30. *See also* Advisers; Advising programs
Academic alert system, 110
Academic and social systems, 24–26
Accessibility of advising systems, 50–53
Adjustment difficulties, student, 26 Admissions: intrusive advising during, 98
Adult learners, 30; part-time student, 75–76, 107–108; student development into, 22–23; theories on, 14
Adviser training. *See* Programs, adviser training; Training of advisers
Advisers: areas of assessment of, 64–65; awards for, 70, 72; class and race values of, 85–87, 89–90; evaluation for, 38–39, 43–44, 73; job satisfaction among, 109; literature on, 106–107, 108–109; maturity of, 8; methods for evaluating, 67–69; multicultural sensitivity of, 89–90, 93; professional credibility of, 50–53; recognition and reward for, 40, 44, 69–72; responsibilities and knowledge areas of, 59–61, 106–107; self-appraisal of ethnicity by, 89–90; types and titles of, 34, 35, 50–53. *See also* Academic advisers; Faculty advisers
Advising program content. *See* Topics
Advising programs: components of, 58–61, 65–66; consumerist, 110–111; delivery systems for, 49–53; effectiveness of, 41, 65–66; evaluation by students, 67–69; for first-semester students, 101–103; generic characteristics of, 85; goals of, 40–41; an ideal model of, 53; importance of, 22, 27–28; improvement steps, 108; institutional evaluation of, 38–39, 43–44, 65, 73; intrusive, 97–103, 109–111; literature on organization of, 107–108;

for minority students, 92–93; seven models of, 48–49; status and progress of, 42–44; strategies for advisees, 78–81; and student retention, 22, 26–28, 60, 84; task-focused 0–100 percent method of, 91–92; third world group variables in, 85–86. *See also* Programs, adviser training
African Americans, 84–90; developmental tasks of, 16
Alert system, academic, 110
Allen, D. R., 85
American Association for Counseling and Development, 109
American College Testing (ACT) national surveys on academic advising, 64; commentary on, 33–41; fourth annual, 33–44; institutions in, 33–34; results, 33–41
American College Testing (ACT) Program, 28, 44, 47, 64, 108, 111
American Council on Education, 83
Articulation agreements, student transfer, 29, 76, 77
Asian students: advising, 84–90
Assessment of advising. *See* Evaluation programs
Assessment of students: intrusive advising and, 98–99, 107
Associate degrees: achievement of, 75–76, 77
Associations, professional, 111
Astin, A. W., 83, 84, 92
Atkinson, D. R., 88, 89
Attneave, C., 87
Authority figures, attitudes toward: by students of color, 97; by women, 15
Awards for recognition of advisers, 70, 72

Banning, M. F., 7, 13
Beal, P. E., 28
Belcher, M. J., 110
Belenky, M. F., 15
Bernal, G., 87
Between-semesters advising, 103
Black students: advising, 16, 84–90

113

# ORDERING INFORMATION

NEW DIRECTIONS FOR COMMUNITY COLLEGES is a series of paperback books that provides expert assistance to help community colleges meet the challenges of their distinctive and expanding educational mission. Books in the series are published quarterly in Spring, Summer, Fall, and Winter and are available for purchase by subscription and individually.

SUBSCRIPTIONS for 1993 cost $48.00 for individuals (a savings of more than 20 percent over single-copy prices) and $70.00 for institutions, agencies, and libraries. Please do not send institutional checks for personal subscriptions. Standing orders are accepted.

SINGLE COPIES cost $15.95 when payment accompanies order. (California, New Jersey, New York, and Washington, D.C., residents please include appropriate sales tax.) Billed orders will be charged postage and handling.

DISCOUNTS for quantity orders are available. Please write to the address below for information.

ALL ORDERS must include either the name of an individual or an official purchase order number. Please submit your order as follows:
Subscriptions: specify series and year subscription is to begin
Single copies: include individual title code (such as CC1)

MAIL ALL ORDERS TO:
Jossey-Bass Publishers
350 Sansome Street
San Francisco, California 94104

FOR SINGLE-COPY SALES OUTSIDE OF THE UNITED STATES CONTACT:
Maxwell Macmillan International Publishing Group
866 Third Avenue
New York, New York 10022

FOR SUBSCRIPTION SALES OUTSIDE OF THE UNITED STATES, contact any international subscription agency or Jossey-Bass directly.

OTHER TITLES AVAILABLE IN THE
NEW DIRECTIONS FOR COMMUNITY COLLEGES SERIES
*Arthur M. Cohen,* Editor-in-Chief
*Florence B. Brawer,* Associate Editor